Books by Frederick Buechner

Novels

Non-Fiction

GODRIC

Frederick Buechner

G O D R I C

Atheneum New York 1980

Library of Congress Cataloging in Publication Data

Buechner, Frederick, 1926–
    Godric.

    1. Godric, Saint, d. 1170—Fiction.
I. Title.
PZ3.B8597Go   1980   [PS3552.U35]   813'.54
ISBN 0–689–11086–3   80–66014

Published simultaneously in Canada by McClelland
and Stewart Ltd.
Manufactured by American Book–Stratford Press
Saddle Brook, New Jersey
Designed by Harry Ford
First Edition

IN MEMORIAM PATRIS MEI
ET AD MAIOREM DEI GLORIAM
ATQUE SANCTI GODRICI

Contents

GODRIC

Of Godric, his friends, and Reginald.

Five friends I had, and two of them snakes. Tune
and Fairweather they were, thick round as a
man's arm, my bedmates and playfellows, keepers
of my skimped hearth and hermit's heart till in a
grim pet I bade them go that day and nevermore
to come again, nevermore to hiss their snakelove
when they saw me drawing near or coil themselves
for warmth about my shaggy legs. They went. They
never came again.

I spied them now and then, puddling my way
home like a drowned man from dark Wear with
my ballocks shriveled to beansize in their sack and
old One-eye scarce a barnacle's length clear of my
belly and crying a-mercy. It was him as I sought
in freezing Wear to teach a lesson that he never
learned nor has to this day learned though wiser,
you'd think, for sixty winters' dunking in bone-
chilling, treacherous Wear. Not him. I would spy
my gentle Tune and watchdog, firetooth Fairweather watching me as still as death in the long
grass or under a stone as I hied home sodden on
cracked feet, but none of us ever let on that we were
seeing what we saw until we saw no longer. I miss
them no more or hardly do, past most such sweet
grieving now at age above a hundred if I've got
time straight for once. For old Godric's now more

3

dead than quick, a pile of dark rags left to steam and scorch now by the fire. It's the missing them now I miss.

That's two. The third was Roger Mouse, as stout of heart and limb as foul of mouth, plowing the stormy seas for pilfer or prize. He had an eye out ever for the willing maids, and no matter to Mouse were they flaxenlocked Dane or black Spaniard, old as earth or cherryripe for the plucking. No matter to Mouse if the deck was awash and storm in the rigging. He'd play with them at diddelydum the weather be damned and cared not a pin that the eyes of the oars were upon them. What a man was Mouse! What a sinner too was Mouse, but none was ever a fonder friend, and what with all the man's great mirth, there was less room left in him for truly mortal sin than in your landlocked, penny-pinching chapmen working their cheerless stealth at the fairs where we peddled.

We had rabbitfur, goosefeather, beeswax, calfskin, garlic and gauds galore. We'd load them cheap the one place and unload them dear the other for any fatrump mistress or dungfoot pilgrim with cockles in his hat that had the pence to squander. We grew rich till one fine day the *Saint Esprit* was ours with her sharp prow that sliced the waves like cheese. Mouse stood so high he said it blew the caps off men who stood astern when he broke wind. Godric was captain helmsman with a canny nose for weather, and captain Mouse was Godric's charm against the Evil Eye, for, mark you, Mouse's sin smacked less of evil than of larkishness the likes of which Our Lord himself could hardly help but wink at when he spied it out in whore and prodigal.

I loved Mouse. Together we saved a Christian

king from infidels and not a silver coin to split between us for our pains. Years afterward, two hundred miles and more away in my dry hut, I saw Mouse in the eye of my heart go down with *Saint Esprit* off the Welsh rocks. He cried out the only name he knew me by, which was not Godric, and in the ear of my heart I heard him, helpless.

Ailred was fourth. They say as a babe he reared up like a lily in his tub and spoke the *Pater Noster* through nor would take of his mother's teat for the forty days and nights of Lent save Sabbaths. He grew to a sheaf of bones made fast round the middle with a monk's rope.

The pictish king of Galloway was the devil fleshed. He had the gold eyes of a toad and a forked beard. On cold nights he'd slit a slave's belly open like a sack so he could dabble his feet in the warm bowels. He tied together the limbs of women in labor for sport and drank blood. Ailred went to him. Throned on a rock, the king was picking his teeth with the bone of a weasel when Ailred knelt and watered his shins with tears. They say a light went forth from Ailred then that blinded the king's gold eyes, and a creature was seen passing forth out of the king hung all over with bottles of the blood he'd drunk, and the king swore holy faith from that day on and took him the name of Ailred for his own. Thus with no loss of seed or purity, my friend got him a son that day upon the rock, and Jesu a forkbeard, pictish knight though blind as a bat from that day on.

Ailred himself they made abbot after a time at Rievaulx where so great was his meekness the fat monks vied with each other to try it till one day one of them, finding him flat in a swoon from an attack of the stone, plucked him up as weighed no more than the weight of his thin bones and cast him onto the fire. But Ailred forgave him, wouldn't you know. He'd let them harm no hair of the monk's head for the mischief he'd done. Nor was Ailred himself so much as singed.

He visits me from time to time. You'd never take him for holy. He smells of fish, his smock hiked up to his hips and his long legs lank as a heron's as he picks his way along the banks of Wear coughing his fearsome cough.

"Peace, Godric," he says.

He's all bones. Godric's all rags. They kneel there hours on end under the low thatch without a word to clutter the silence save for the prayers they heave heavenward braided together like a hawser the better to hoist the world a cat's whisker out of the muck. Only once did he do me a bad turn, and that was from love as many a bad turn's been done from before. He sent me Reginald.

"To put your life on parchment, Godric," Ailred says. His cough's like the splitting of wood. "To un-bushel the light of your days for the schooling of children. To set them a path to follow." Did he but know where Godric's path has led or what sights his light has lit, he'd bushel me back fast enough. I've told Mother Reginald tales to rattle his beads and blush his fishbelly tonsure pink as a babe's bum, but he turns them all to treacle with his scratching quill. I scoop out the jakes of my remembrance, and he censes it all with his clerkish screed till it reeks of mass. He brings me broth and plovers' eggs. He freshens my straw when I foul it. If some dream shipwrecks me at night, he's there with his taper to beacon me safe to shore. Just the sight of his sheep-face gives me the cramp.

I lie with my eyes rolled back to the whites and my jaws agape so he'll think I'm a corpse before he's dug his book from me. Often I speak to him only with the tongue of my hands which he does not understand. I have taught rats to run over him in the dark. But I suffer him. For it was lowly, gentle, dark-eyed Ailred sent him.

The fifth was Gillian. I met her on a Roman hill with Aedwen, my mother, drowsing at my side. She journeyed in our pilgrim band. At each day's end she'd bathe my feet. She crept beneath my cloak.

I have forgotten my father's face. I have forgotten my own face when I was young. By God's mercy someday I will forget Reginald's face. But her face I'll remember ever. Gillian I will not forget.

That's five friends, one for each of Jesu's wounds, and Godric bears their mark still on what's left of him as in their time they all bore his on them. What's friendship, when all's done, but the giving and taking of wounds?

When Godric banished Fairweather and Tune, they all three bled for it, and part of Godric snaked off too nevermore to come again. And it's Godric's flesh that Ailred's cough cleaves like an axe. And when brave Mouse went down off Wales, he bore to the bottom the cut of Godric's sharp farewell. And when Gillian vanished in a Dover wood, she took with her all but the husk of Godric's joy.

Gentle Jesu, Mary's son, be thine the wounds that heal our wounding. Press thy bloody scars to ours

7

that thy dear blood may flow in us and cleanse our sin.

Be thou in us and we in thee that Godric, Gillian, Ailred, Mouse and thou may be a woundless one at last. And even Reginald if thy great mercy reach so far.

In God's name Godric prays. Amen.

*Of the family of Godric, his youth, and a
sign from the sea.*

AEDLWARD the freeman was my father, and Reginald has it that his name means Keeper of
Blessedness. If so, he kept it mostly to himself, more's
the pity. I pity Aedlward. If he pitied me, he never
said.

Aedlward's face I've long since lost, but his back
I can still behold. He held his head cocked sideways, and his ears stood out like handles on a pot
as he strode forth from the smoke of our hut to
work our own scant croft of leeks, parsley, shallots,
and the like, or else my lord's wide acres. Endless
was the work there was, the seeding, the spreading
of dung, reaping and threshing, cutting and storing.
In winter there were scythes and plows to mend,
the beasts to keep, roofs to patch until your fingers
froze. It seems that he was ever striding off in every
way but ours so I scarcely had the time to mark the
smile or scowl of him. Even the look of his eyes is
gone. They were grey as the sea like mine, it's said,
only full of kindness, but what matter how kind a
man's eye be if he never fixes you with it long
enough to learn?

He had a way of whistling through his teeth like

9

wind through wattle, and it's like wind that I remember him. His was a power to thump doors open and shut like wind, a grey gust of a man to make flames fly and scatter chaff. But wind has no power to comfort a child or lend a strong arm to a lad whose bones are weak with growing. If Aedlward and Godric meet in Paradise, they'll meet as strangers do and never know.

It was fear kept Aedlward from us, and next to God what he feared of all things most was an empty belly. He had good cause. He had seen poor famished folk eat rat and cat and seen grown men suckle their wives for strength enough to ferret nuts to feed them. Bitterer fare than that a man will go to when his belly starts to gnaw itself. So it was his fear we'd starve that made him starve us for that one of all things that we hungered for the most, which was the man himself.

The man was ever leaving us. If my lord said harrow, he'd harrow, said tinker, he'd tinker or fettle he'd fettle though he was no villein bound to serve but a man born free as any man and paid the rent of our poor roof with pence. But my lord was all there was to save us if the harvest failed, so if the hens no longer sat, I think my father would have laid an egg himself to please my lord. He loved us sure, but like the bread a beggar dreams, his love could never pad the ribs or make the heart grow strong.

I sometimes see him to this day in dreams. He sits by the hearth, his back as ever turned. His chin has fallen to his chest. He neither sleeps nor wakes. There's a sack of onions on his knee, and his hands hang dark from grubbing in the earth. I huddle close to him to turn him by his great cold ears so I can see him plain at last. But Godric's hands close ever shut on empty air, and even in his dreams that face escapes.

But Aedwen, my mother, there's another tale. Friend of Blessedness, says scrivener Reginald, and, blessed or not, she was a friend to all. What a lass she must have been with her hair in a braid and her rosy cheeks though it's never as a lass that a man remembers the mother that bore him. I remember her leading a Christmas jig in the churchyard, though, till Tom Ball the priest flew out to scold.

God in his wrath might keep them jigging the whole year through, Ball said, till they'd jigged to the depths of their waists in the sod. But *Sweetheart, have pity* they went on singing all Christmas Eve till so wrought was poor Ball that he stammered it forth the next morning at mass. "Sweetheart, have pity," he said when he should have said, "Jesu, have mercy."

How Aedwen stuffed her braid in her mouth at that! Or she'd cover her mirth with her hands and shake till you'd think that the fit was upon her. She did the same too when she wept so you'd never be sure which she hid with her hands, her tears or her cackling. I think there were times she herself didn't know, nor does anyone know at times. Laugh till you weep. Weep till there's nothing left but to laugh at your weeping. In the end it's all one.

It was Burcwen, my sister, that tried her most. Burcwen had ears like Aedlward's which she bound with a cloth at night to lay them flat. It never did. She had long legs and hair in a tangle and a gap between her teeth for squirting cider or perry through if ever the whim should take her. You never knew. She could outrun, outjig, outdevil the lads, and it was lads' toil and lads' sport she fancied. She'd have none of spinning with the women and Aedwen. She loathed staining my lord's wool with woad or vermillion, and her loaves were hard and flat as tiles. Aedwen would box her big ears and Aedlward take a rope to her if he'd strength enough left from his grubbing, but it was no use. Off she'd flee to hunt coney again or bedevil the ox with his great saint's eye.

Burcwen loved the lads, but it was like another lad herself she loved them. I think she was twelve before she learned they carried under their clothes what she herself was clean without. And when they found her flesh sweet and tried to tumble her, it sent her into a terrible fright and puzzle for thinking she wasn't a lass nor a lad either. There was nothing left for her to be but only Burcwen. So only Burcwen she was, lonely Burcwen, merry and larkish yet but in her own freaked fashion. She'd harry geese and climb high branches. She'd set the swine loose in Tom Ball's garden. She'd tease the hot lads in a way not to flame but to quench them, she thought, mocking their barnyard lust with speech ruder far than any they knew themselves how to muster. Then Aedwen would cover her face with her hands and toss to and fro like a windy tree. Brother William was Burcwen's one fast friend till brother Godric stole her off.

Godric was older than either with a breach of years between that came of a stillbirth and several small deaths no whit less still. Aedwen had hardly been delivered of William when she waxed great with Burcwen, and the two of them grew up like finger and thumb at first. They made a wry pair. Burcwen was merry and mad. Burcwen was Burcwen. William was owlish from the day he was born.

When William fixed you with his great round eye, you felt he knew when last you'd done the deed of darkness and the one you'd done it with and where. When Aedlward brought apples or onions back, William would count them out to the last one and any day you liked could tell the number left. And how the boy could talk!

Words came spilling out of him before he knew their meaning, and if there was none to listen, he'd talk to his own ten toes. He didn't care a fig for what he talked about. One matter would serve him as well as another. He'd prattle of Normans or crops or weather till the spittle gathered at the corners of his mouth, and if you made a move to flee, there'd come to his eyes a haunted look, and he'd prattle all the faster so you'd find no chink to flee him through. Words were the line that moored him to the world, I think, and he thought if ever the line should break, he'd be forever cast adrift.

Burcwen was his chief mooring at the start. Day after day they'd sit at sundown on a stile, their faces dark against the crimson sky, and William ever buzzing in her ear. I don't think Burcwen paid much mind to what he said, but the sound alone worked some spell on her the way they say that music will on beasts. It soothed and rested her at least. It gave her peace to gather back the bits and pieces of herself the day had scattered. And I think that William scarcely listened to himself or cared if she paid heed or not, for it wasn't her heed he sought for with his words. It was herself to make fast to against the world's wild winds that sought to blow him out to sea for drowning. The jest of it was that Godric was the one that almost drowned.

It happened thus. I was a lad of twenty-odd and William and Burcwen both but children still. I was off in the fens one April day to set out snares for waterfowl not far from where the Welland flows into the Wash. A stiff breeze blew across the saltings, and the air was watery chill. I see it yet and yet see Godric seeing it as well.

He was full of glee and daring then with a boy's heart still in the downy breast of a man. His neck hadn't thickened yet, nor his chest swelled to a tun, nor his nose fleshed out to the great hook it became, but a bird's beak then. He had the seagrey eyes of Aedlward although with less of kindness in them than a bird's cold glint and cunning. His beard was sparse and short, not yet the great black pricklebush it later grew. His raven hair fell shoulderlong, and save for a skin tied round his waist, he was naked as Father Adam was before his shame. Nor yet knew Godric shame himself. A young beast, sure, but with a beast's young innocence.

Then far out across the shingle where skycolored sand and water meet, he spied a shape. Something glittered humped and wet there like a wrecked craft's cargo or a pirate's carcase sewn with gold along the seams or something rarer yet washed up from ancient Roman times, for legend is that Caesar drained old Wash to plow like meadowland and buried treasure there. Through the shallows Godric raced, birdbeaked, his arms stretched out like wings. Splashing silver spray chest-high, he was soaked to the bone but never even felt the chill, his blood so full of flame. It was only a fish when he reached it, but ah, such a fish it was!

Blackbacked and blunt of snout, it lay on its side with its belly glinting in the sun like pearl. Its mouth grinned wide in welcome. Its porpoise eyes were glazed and gay in death. Salted down, it would have served to feed a family all through spring or more, so Godric with his knife set in to gutting it. This was no easy task, for the fish was longer than a man and of a heft to match. Godric's blade was slight, and just to cut the thews and bones that held the head took time. Thus he did not mark the freshening of the breeze and the tide's swift turning till he glanced to find himself upon a spit of sand ringed round with scudding waves.

But still there was much work to do. He scoured the empty belly clean with brine. He lopped the tail and great three-cornered fin. At last he was left with a hundredweight of fillet which he laid across his shoulders so that like a bishop's stole it hung down low to either side. Then up to his breast in surf he started for the shore.

It boiled him like a turnip in a broth. It knocked him off his feet and pounded him. When he opened up his mouth to cry, it filled his mouth. His burden dragged him under, yet he would not let it go, for though the deep churned dark about him, still deeper in his heart he saw that porpoise eye so blithe in death and heard its voice, or so he thought, say, "Take and eat me, Godric, to thy soul's delight. Hold fast to him who gave his life for thee and thine." Godric's breath then failed him. He was sucked down by the tide.

Burcwen found him. He awoke upon the strand to find her lips on his to breathe life back in him. His head was cradled in her lap. All said it was a miracle, and so I think it may have been.

Three lessons Godric learned that day.

The first was that the sea's a killer, nor did he ever from that day forget nor fail again to keep an eye cocked on the waves' salt treachery.

The second was he learned that Burcwen's heart was his. Less and less as months passed by did she seek William out or sit astride their sundown stile to hear him buzz his need at her. More and more it was Godric that she sought for soothing, and he her. They spoke but little. Once she laid her fingers on his lips and said it was her breath they breathed. Who knows but it was so?

Lesson three was that he learned whose voice he'd heard beneath the waves and whose the eye that gazed at him so merrily. He learned that it was Jesu saved him from the sea, though saved him why or saved for what deep end he did not learn, nor has he ever learned it to this day.

*How Reginald asked and Godric answered
and the Blessed Virgin's song.*

"AEDWEN named you well, Father," says Reginald in his coddling lilt.

I say, "Father my bum."

"A holy name for a babe born to be holy," he says.

"Fiddle my faddle," I say or nothing at all in words but something instead in the fingertalk he doesn't know. He's better off not knowing, if he only knew.

"The *god* means *God*. That's plain as your nose, I mean no slight. The *ric* is Saxon *reign*. So *God* and *ric* in sum means God reigns, Godric. It means God reigns in you. It means when God comes down at last to weigh the souls of men, he'll not find Godric's wanting, Father Godric."

"Fetch me a bowl to puke in," I tell him. He's got him such a honeyed way I'm ever out to sour it.

"Godric will have his little jest," says Reginald.

So then I teach him other ways to read my name. *"God's god* for sure. You hit that square. But *ric* is Erse for *wreck,"* I say, not knowing Erse from arse. "God's wreck I be, it means. God's wrecked Godric for his sins. Or Godric's sins have made a wreck of God."

17

Reginald throws up his hands, his palms as pale and soft as cheese.

"There's other ways as well," I say. "Rip Godric up another seam, and what you get is *go* and *drick*."

"What's *drick*?" says Reginald.

"A foul Welsh word not fit for monkish ears," I say.

"How great is your *humilitas,* Father," Reginald says.

I say, "Yet, Mother, not so great as is my drick."

Why is it that the best in him calls forth the worst in me?

"When were you born, Father?" he says.

"The year of my birth."

"What manner of man is John the Baptist when he visits you in dreams?"

"Something between a goat and a Jew."

"Is it true you see what's happening years ahead and miles away, Father?"

"I see a man and maid a-tumble on your grave."

"They say the Blessed Virgin taught you songs."

I open my mouth and croak like one who's had his tongue snipped out for swearing false. *Eck, eck,* I sing, twiddling my eyelids like a beggar playing blind.

When was I born? They say it was the year before the Bastard William beached his Normans at Pevensey, slaying Harold with a sunset shaft shot through his eye, then stomping down the golden Wessex dragon in the mud. They tell that Harold's mother said she'd give its weight in gold to have the body of her son laid deep in holy ground, but William buried it instead in Saxon soil that Harold hallowed by his falling there. Then William up and had them crown him king at Westminster on

Christmas day, and when the Aethling joined with Dane and Scot to cast him out, stark William marched his Normans north and harried the land from sea to sea. Men, women, children, all, he put them to the sword in bitter cold. He slew their beasts and burned their crops and set aflame their towns until the folk cried mercy and the land was his. Thus Godric first saw light at a dark time, and the manger of his birth was death.

But all is light for Reginald. What do they know of dark and death, he and his brother Durham monks? Saint Benedict would twitch inside his tomb to see them water down his rule. No wonder that the hands of monks are soft the way they've got them brewers, barbers, tailors, cooks to do their bidding and husbandmen to work their soil. No meat for monks unless they ail, says Benedict, so half the monks and more plead sick each day and gather in the misericorde to stuff their mouths with mutton till the fat runs down. The Loft, they call it, and mighty high and lofty are their ways. They copy their books and say their prayers, and if some wandering duke or prince comes by, they turn their cloisters to an inn to please his grace and bend their knees as deep as if to kiss my lord the bishop's ring.

And it's this same soft Reginald that asks of John the Baptist, what I've seen of him in dreams. I've seen a man all clad in rags and anger still although a kinsman of Our Lord as well as a high saint. I've seen a shaft of light aslant through dark, a fierce lance tilted to the heart of things, a flail, a knout. How do you tell of such a one as John to such as Reginald, who'd have him be a godly gelding like himself? "Abide alone," John told me once. "Make thy place in wilderness as I did mine that the

Lord may house thee. Make roots and grubs thy only fare that the Lord may feed thee. Make chilly Wear thy Jordan that the Lord may warm thee. Thus friendless, roofless, blue with cold, yet singing praise, the world may learn of thee the glory and the grace of God."

I say, "Mark me now, Reginald. Hear this."

He sets down the eggs he's brought and squats beside me in the straw so he may catch the words he thinks will come out weak because he thinks that Godric's weak and old as Adam's shoe.

"WRITE THIS DOWN IN YOUR BOOK!" I cry with all the strength I have. Then see him clap his hands to his ears and rock back on his heels. But then he rocks back close again, for when I speak a second time, I barely mumble in my beard. Thus I play him like a fish. He looks a fish. His mouth's agape. His eyes are flat.

I say, "Then if you want it, here's my life." You'd think it was the sacrament I tendered him, the seemly way he bows his head to hear.

I say, "I started out as rough a peasant's brat and full of cockadoodledoo as any. I worked uncleanness with the best of them or worst. I tumbled all the maids would suffer me and some that scratched and tore like weasels in a net. I planted horns on many a goodman's brow and jollied lads with tales about it afterward. I took up peddling as my trade. I cozened and tricked the way a baker yeasts his loaves till they are less of bread than air. I passed off old for new. I let out pence at usury. I swore me false. A flatterer I was. A wanderer. I thieved and pirated. I went to sea. Such things as happened then are better left unsaid."

Reginald's eyes are rolled up in his head so all

that shows is white. He crosses himself and like a herring in a basket gasps for air. Yet I've spared him things far worse for the sake of sparing Godric too. I've spared him wasted Burcwen nibbling like a hare on grass and leaves. I've spared him William calling out along the darkened banks of Wear for what he'll never find. I've spared him two that lay as one in one another's arms and never spoke a word.

"There's much you're better not to know," I say, "but know you this. Know Godric's no true hermit but a gadabout within his mind, a lecher in his dreams. Self-seeking he is and peacock proud. A hypocrite. A ravener of alms and dainty too. A slothful, greedy bear. Not worthy to be called a servant of the Lord when he treats such servants as he has himself like dung, like Reginald. All this and worse than this go say of Godric in your book."

Poor Reginald's tears run trickling down his cheeks like tallow. He asks for sweet, and bitter's all he has from me. Have I no honeyed crumb to take the taste away?

"Well, but say this also if you like," I say. "Say yes, it's true that Mary came. She came though who knows why. Clad all in skyblue mantling with the crown of Heaven on her head. She smiled at me."

And then I raised up on one elbow in the straw and sang:

> *Saint, Mary, virgin dame.*
> *Mother of Jesu Christ, of God his Lamb,*
> *Take, shield, and do thy Godric bring*
> *To thee where Christ is King.*
> *Our Lady, maiden, springtime's flower,*
> *Deliver Godric from this hour.*

For Ailred's sake I sang it to the monk he sent.
And what I said to him is so. It was indeed the
Blessed Virgin taught it me.

How Godric left home.

"FAREWELL, Father. Mother, farewell," I said.
Aedwen took and slowly turned my face
from side to side as if to rummage it for something
there she'd lost or feared to lose. She gave me a
sack of berries and a wool cap. She wept no tears,
and not a word came from her lips.

Aedlward, my father, was sitting by the fire. He
did not rise. He only raised one hand, then spoke
the only word of all the words he ever spoke to me
that I remember still as his.

"You'll have your way, Godric," he said, and to
this day that word he spoke and that raised hand
are stitched together in my mind.

I believe my way went from that hand as a path
goes from a door, and though many a mile that
way has led me since, with many a turn and cross-
road in between, if ever I should trace it back, it's
to my father's hand that it would lead. I kissed him
on his head then, for he'd turned away to watch the
flames. He smelled of oxen and of rain. It was the
last I ever saw of him.

Tom Ball came by to bless me. Ball was a heavy,
slow-paced man who had one eye that veered off on
a starboard tack so you never knew for sure which
way he looked. He entered our house splashed high

with mud, for our yard was always a bog through spring. He sweated like a horse.

He laid his hands on me and blessed my eyes to see God's image deep in every man. He blessed my ears to hear the cry especially of the poor. He blessed my lips to speak no word but Gospel truth. He warned against the Devil and his snares with always that one eye of his skewed off as if to watch for snares himself.

"This life of ours is like a street that passes many doors," Ball said, "nor think you all the doors I mean are wood. Every day's a door and every night. When a man throws wide his arms to you in friendship, it's a door he opens same as when a woman opens hers in wantonness. The street forks out, and there's two doors to choose between. The meadow that tempts you rest your bones and dream a while. The rackribbed child that begs for scraps the dogs have left. The sea that calls a man to travel far. They all are doors, some God's and some the Fiend's. So choose with care which ones you take, my son, and one day—who can say—you'll reach the holy door itself."

"Which one is that, Father?" I asked for courtesy, for I was hot to leave. I was on my knees before him and with his one straight eye he held me there.

"Heaven's door, Godric," he said.

"And will I know it if I reach that far?"

"Perhaps you won't," Ball said. "Perhaps you will. But go now, Godric. The peace of God go with you too. Tom Ball will keep you in his prayers."

So if my father's hand is the door from which my way went forth, please God the door it leads me to may be the one Saint Peter keeps. And blessed be he who knows it when he comes to it,

24

for not all do, I think. Often when my way has led me not to the great door itself, God knows, but past some little glimpse of it, it wasn't for years I knew the worth of what I'd glimpsed, and then too late. Fool that I was, I thought that day that it was only home I left.

The only one who wept was he who had least cause for tears, and that was William. He'd have crowed like a cock on a dunghill if he'd been anybody else, for now with Godric going off, Burcwen would be his again. How he must have missed her those last years! Ever since that day she found me on the sands of Wash half-drowned and loved me for the breath she'd breathed into my lips, he'd been busy as a sailor in a gale to find some other place to moor.

With Burcwen gone, he'd searched to find some other friend. Old folk he'd tried with nothing else to do, he thought, but please a lad like him, and younger folk he hoped would have him and be proud, and others his same age to play with at bowls and stick-and-stone. But in the end his endless chatter drove them all away. Nor young nor old had time enough for the time that William needed nor room in their heart's quiet for one who never could be still. Yet now, though Godric's leaving gave him Burcwen back, he wept to see him go.

As I passed the lower sheepfold, I found Burcwen waiting there. She had no cloak nor shoes upon her feet but carried a basket on her arm.

"I'm going with thee, Godric," she said.

I said, "And so's the Man in the Moon thine uncle, child."

The wind blew rain about, and my lord's fat sheep were huddled with their backs to it. Against her cheek, my sister's hair was wet, and there was wildness in her eye.

"See what I've got," she said and from her basket drew a length of hemp. "Unless I go, I'll hang myself. They'll bury me at the crossroads with a stake drove through my heart."

I said, "Just standing out here in the rain you'll catch your death."

"It's my life I'm here to catch before it gets away," she said. "My life's with you, Godric."

"And so is mine with you," I said, "and one day I'll come back with wealth enough to build us a great house where we'll live out our days in peace."

"The Man in the Moon must be your uncle too," she said.

"But for now, your life is here," I said, "and my life's mine to find and fashion where I may. So Godric goes," I said, "and Burcwen stays." I raised her chin so she could read the firmness in my face. "Dear heart, farewell," I said, and when I left, she made no move to follow me.

After I had gone some fifty paces, though, I heard her calling through the wind. With a lad's quick skill, she'd shinnied up a tree and tied one rope-end fast around a branch and with the other sought to make a hangman's knot.

"Stay see me jump!" she called, then something else the wind blew off. I saw she laughed, and laughter too was part of what was choking me, but there was madness in our mirth, for I was daring her to die and Burcwen daring me to drive her to. So then I ran to save her while I still had time.

I plucked her off her branch like a treed cat, and we scuffled, laughing in the rain, while I trussed her underneath the arms and hoisted her until she hung there dangling from her tree again. When she saw that there was nothing she could do, she went so grave and still she could have been an angel overhead. Her virgin breasts were bared where she had torn her clothes, her head a flower bending on its stem.

"Look in the basket, Godric," she said in a small voice, "and take the parting gift I brought."

It was a cross she'd whittled from two bits of wood and bound with strands of her own hair. I hung it round my neck, and there it hangs still to this day, the hair as bright and soft as it was then.

"You've foxed me fair this time," she said, "but other times will come and slyer foxes."

"And so they will," I said.

"Farewell then, Godric," she said from where she hung. She wanly flapped her arms at me like wings. "May the Man in the Moon watch over you till next we meet."

I've wondered since if maybe why she brought that rope was not to hang herself but so I'd have the means to make her stay. I think that in some corner of her heart she wanted to be bound against her own wild will to go with me as in the wilds of me I yearned to cut her down so she could come.

But off I went and never gave another backward glance lest like Lot's wife I'd turn into a pillar salt as my own tears.

Of Peregrine Small and how Godric came to prosper in trade.

I think of Fairweather and Tune, of Fairweather with his tongue of flame and sleepy, faithful Tune. Have they withstood the years? Do they drape themselves like garlands over dead limbs still and coil themselves for sun on rocks too high for Wear to wet? Have they found it in their hearts to pardon Godric?

If they but knew, it was not the coldness but the warmth of Godric's bowels for them that made him drive them off. It's hard to fasten on the airy love of God when such as earthy Tune with jewels for eyes slips on his belly through the dust to pay his loving court. Tune slept in a jar, but at my every entering he'd rear his head and shuttle to and fro to weave my welcome.

Fairweather guarded me. Whenever a man drew near, or monk or maid, he was fierce to strike and swift to sting. The trouble was he guarded me from God as well. Let God himself approach me down the path I made of prayers, and such a hissing would break forth from Fairweather then you would have thought the King of Glory was my foe. For love of me, Fairweather warded off the love of God, and since I loved Fairweather for his care, I had to banish him with Tune.

I paid a smith to fettle me from the lids of two great pots the iron vest I wear to fret the devil in my flesh, and when I walk, it sounds to warn the world I'm near the way that Ailred's cough warns me of him. Do my snake friends listen still for Godric clanking through the trees, or Godric's clank and Ailred's cough like the chanting back and forth of monks at mass? Does Godric listen still for them? He listens surely. There's no doubt of that. But ah, there are so many sounds!

All those years ago Tom Ball blessed my ears to hear the poor cry out for help, and I still hear them right enough. I hear them when the mouse squeals in the owl's cruel claw. I hear them when the famished wolf howls hunger at the moon. I hear them when old Wear goes rattling past in weariness, and in the keening of the wind, and when the rain beats hollow on my roof. In all such sounds I hear the poor folk's bitter need and in the dimtongued silence too. But when melody wells up in thrushes' throats, and bees buzz honeysong, and rock and river clap like hands in summer sun, then misery's drowned in minstrelsy, and Godric's glad in spite of all. Yet sometimes too he's sad in spite of all, God knows, for there are other voices than the poor's.

One is the voice of Peregrine Small, a weaver late of Bishop's Lynn, where I went to peddle at the fair not many months from when I left my sister dangling like a Christmas goose. Small's cloth was of a weft so fine you could have pulled it through a lady's ring, and he himself was scarce less dainty. He had a man's parts and a silken yellow beard, but when he walked, he swayed his hams from side to side, and when he opened up his bearded lips, it was the simper of a maid came forth.

Poor Small, he could not help himself. He didn't paint his face like some I've seen nor seek out men to use him for a maid, but Mistress Small they called him, and the lads were always making sport of him to see him blush and roll his cow-eyes heavenward. It's the voice of this same Small that echoes still in Godric's ears. *E-e-e-e-e-k! E-e-e-e-e-k!* he cried as if they sought to ravish him, and in the knock-kneed manner of a maid fled down Saint Margaret's darkling nave.

It happened thus. It was fair time, as I say. The town was full. Merchants were there from many parishes with tents and stalls and painted flags, and others from as far away as Flanders with their wines, dyes, hides, furs, herbs and wares of every sort too rare to name. Cattle and swine thronged through the streets till you walked up to your shins in dung. Notaries were busy with their wax to seal contracts and bargains, and whores flocked everywhere to seal some bargains of their own wherever there were walls or bits of ground left dry enough to prop their bums against Jack Ploughman's huff and puff. From miles around the rich and poor alike came out to gawk at dogs in kerchiefs standing on their heads or bears that jigged and one sick lion riding on a sumpter mule, his great tongue lolling. Magicians drew live doves out of the air as easy as thimble-riggers drew pence out of dunces' pockets, and the Jews in their horned caps and yellow badges sat in booths to weigh out silver at the rates of gold.

A Jew named Haggai sparked the tinder of that moiling time. As chance would have it, in years and heft he was about the same as Peregrine Small, and like Small too he had a yellow, silken beard. Haggai turned Christian, that's where it began. Perhaps he turned to Jesu truly in his heart, ruing the bloody mischief of the cross the Jews had wrought. Perhaps it was because he was so fair of hair and face he hoped in time to pass for Saxon. Perhaps, since nothing human's not a broth of false and true, it was the two at once.

In any case no less a high and mighty lord would be the one to baptize him than Ranulf Flambard, Chancellor, who'd traveled north to do the business of the king. King William Redhead's business ever was to milk the land of gold and silver till it cried for mercy, and Flambard, called the Torch, was he that pulled the teats for him till they hung dry. Flambard was as sharp a rogue as ever broke wind in a mitre, nor was this the last that Godric heard of him, for their sails were set on courses doomed to cross again. But one day's evil is enough each day, and that day's sprang from Haggai's hallowing.

The Jews caught scent of it and flew into a heathen rage. They wanted Haggai's blood for playing false, and to draw it they were hot to batter down Saint Margaret's door. This door was bolted fast against the hurly-burly of the fair, but the Jews thumped on it with their fists and feet and pikes till all the Christian folk within believed their hour had come and called for help.

What came was more than help or less. Christians came and Jews came, both—magicians, whores and thieves and all who'd traveled to the fair to buy or sell or gawk. Everybody with a nose for heydiddlediddle and danger ran to fill the square, and Godric too, his own great beak a-quiver. He'd bought the hair of women cheap at nunneries where it was cropped and when the ruckus started up was selling it dear to Joans and Jills to plait into their own thin tresses. Saint Margaret's door fell down at last. The crowd pressed in like sheep. And Godric too.

Inside there was a churchly dusk and quiet. Flambard and Haggai both had fled. A flock of Christians cowered around the stoup. A stout priest raised his arms in vain for peace. And then, for want of other foe, the crowd turned on itself. They went to it pellmell. The vengeful Jews were routed soon. Then it was Christian fists that bloodied Christian snouts, and Christian staffs that cracked hard Christian pates like nuts. I myself was mounted on some knightly tomb, crowing like a cock and laying about me with a stick to clobber all who threatened me when all at once I heard a feeble mewing at my feet and turned to find this Peregrine Small crouched down for shelter there behind the tomb.

"Stand up like a man, weaver!" I cried and thwacked him hard across the back to stir him. Puddling the floor for fright, he stood, and, be it ever on my head, a brace of aproned Yorkshire cobblers saw him then and took him with his yellow beard for Haggai.

They set up a cry and in seconds tore the clothes off poor Small's back. They aimed to mock how he was circumcised and work God knows what other mischief on his flesh, and had they only held him long enough to find his parts as whole as theirs, it might have saved his skin. But Small broke free and fled them naked down the nave. His soft flesh flickered white as milk as through Saint Margaret's shade he hooted *e-e-e-e-k!* with what by then was half of Yorkshire on his tail.

He doubled back then as I've seen hares do. Who can say but that he thought to find in me his only friend? And so I might have been indeed, but even as he threw himself into my arms, the pack was on him. The cobblers stabbed him with their awls in throat, breast, belly while Godric, drenched in blood, fell back beneath his broad-beamed, spouting corpse.

The folly of the mob killed Small, and greater follies followed still.

First, word went round it was the Jews that killed him. They said that Small had come upon a Jew dishonoring a Christian tomb and pointed to the puddle Small himself had made to prove that they were right. When Small set out to drive the villain off, they said, six other Jews leapt forth. These six, it seems, the doughty Small did battle with, unaided and unarmed, till one crept up by stealth to pin him from behind while yet another jabbed him in the side just where the Roman lance pierced Christ. Thus weaver Small died Peregrine the Martyr.

Second, they claimed the blood of martyred Small worked miracles. A man born dumb prayed three whole *Aves* through aloud without one fault when but a drop of it was placed upon his tongue. A silver coin that chanced to fall in it was turned to gold, and from the holes the awls had dug, a mist was seen to rise that shaped itself into a holy cross.

Third, there were folk that vied to give as much as six French knives or a pair of ivory combs for a scrap no bigger than a leaf of the garment Small had bled upon. That garment was peddler Godric's own, of course, for Small had bled and died in Godric's arms. He peddled it off in bits and pieces to the last dank thread, then slit a cat's throat on another still and peddled off as much again.

Who knows? He might be peddling cat gore still but that the mighty Flambard called a halt. Already a score or more of Jews had paid for Small's death with their skins, and Flambard feared that as the martyr's fame spread farther yet, more Jews would fall to Christian zeal. He knew that each Jew fallen was a Jew the less to lay a golden egg whenever William Redhead cackled, so Flambard sent the word if Godric wasn't gone from Bishop's Lynn before the sun went down, he'd never see it up again. And Godric went.

He paid for passage on a boat bound north and after three days' up-wind battling reached an isle girt round with cliffs so steep there was no place to moor except an iron ring embedded in the stone. He had them make fast there, then scrambled up the rocks to wait until the boat was gone to work his stealth.

Thus, Master Reginald, set down in your book how it was through a martyr's death that godly Godric's peddling prospered and how the chancellor of an anointed king was the one by whom he first set foot on holy Farne.

How Godric fared on the holy isle of Farne.

HERE is what I found on Farne. I found an old man sleeping on a bed of stone. Campion was everywhere and grey-winged gulls. His lips were still, but had he opened them to speak my name, I think that I'd have followed to the world's far rim. Later, I saw him bent over a spade. I called to him, but he did not even raise his head. When I reached the place where he had stood, I found him gone. I wept and wept I do not know how long. Then as I'd come to do, I buried all my wealth from Bishop's Lynn between a clump of heather and a fish-shaped rock.

I'd brought some cheese but had no stomach for it then. I'd told the boatman I wanted to do penance for my sins and bade him come to fetch me the next day. He said he would. He was a tall, rough fellow with a salty tongue, and yet I knew I trusted him.

Great as my need for penance was, I watched the birds instead. There were black-backed guillemots with crimson feet and gulls and terns so thick you would have thought that Farne itself had wings. The rocks were limed with droppings, the sea air salt and soft with spray. I stood and heard above the surf the creaking sadness of the gulls. A little way apart rose great stone pinnacles like fingers

35

from the sea, some broken off, some with their summits lost in cloud. If Aedlward's had been a giant's hand and turned to stone for birds to nest on, I think it would have looked like that. I wondered if the old man watched it too. That night I saw him yet again.

Whether or not I dreamed, I did not know, but I saw him pick a moonlit path to where I lay and then sit down. He put a finger to his lips and only then I saw he held a sleeping hare with silken ears laid flat against his fur.

"I swooned for hunger once," he said, "and this one stroked me with his tongue until I waked. Glythwin is his name. He shall pray for you, Godric. Perhaps you know that when hares pray, the ears of God grow long as theirs to hear."

"Thank him for me then, Father," I said.

"When hares nip, though, the sting is sharp," he said. "The night I died, they waved lit torches to and fro from that high ledge behind you there to tell my monks on Lindisfarne the news. Would you believe it, though? There was not one of them awake. So Glythwin sank his teeth into the abbot's toe. You should have seen the jig he did with one foot tucked beneath him like a stork!"

"You say that you were dead, and yet you saw?" I said.

"Not only saw but laughed," he said, "till tears ran down."

"Would I be right that you're a ghost then, Father, and you haunt this place?"

"Ah well, and if it comes to that," he said, "your shadow fell here long before your foot, and that's a kind of haunting too. Farne had long been calling you, I mean, before you heard at last and came."

"I heard no call, Father," I said. "I came here as a stranger, and I came by chance."

"Was it as a stranger and by chance you wept?" he said, then let me wonder at his words a while before he spoke again. "When a man leaves home, he leaves behind some scrap of his heart. Is it not so, Godric?"

I thought of Burcwen waiting with her basket in the rain and how I kissed my father's head, and nodded yes.

"It's the same with a place a man is going to," he said. "Only then he sends a scrap of his heart ahead."

"It's true there's something fetching here," I said, "but I had no aim to come, Father, nor have I any aim to stay."

"Nor shall you either," he said. "Your heart's no guillemot to make this isle your rookery. It was right you came to fold your wings a while and get your bearings for the flight to come. But your true nesting place lies farther on."

"Lies where?" I asked.

He said, "Godric, this much at least I know for sure. Until you reach it, every other place you find will fret you like a cage."

The hare had come awake. He raised his ears. The old man set him on the ground. He hopped to where I lay and crouched there with the stars behind his head. I wondered if already he was saying prayers for me and how you prayed with four legs and a tail.

"You know my name, Father," I said. "Now may I ask what yours may be?"

"I never liked it much," he said. "It always makes me think of how a frog sounds plopping in a pond. Cuth-bert! But that's the way they christened me."

"Holy Mother of God!" I cried. "Then you're the holy saint himself!"

"Ah well," he said. "To Gossip Guillemot I'm just a bald head like an egg. To God, who knows?"

Since holiness was all he knew, I think he did not know his own. I went to my knees before him then, for from ancient Saxon times Saint Cuthbert's fame and fear were great.

"Oh forgive me, your worship, for I have sinned," I said. "Bless me, for if I'm not yet damned for good and all, I've only got a spiderleg to go." Then I told him the tale of Peregrine Small and how I slew a cat for blood and sold false relics off for true to honest folk at Bishop's Lynn. My eyes were filled with tears of shame.

For a wonder, it was the cat he asked me of. What manner of cat, he said, and had it suffered cruelly?

"Only a common street cat, sire," I said. "Some bony beggar-cat with ragged ears and twisted tail. As to his suffering, I fear I thought no more of that than of a pig's at sticking time. I think he didn't die at once, but even there I can't be sure."

Cuthbert gave a cry and, gathering up the hare again, knelt down. The moon made silver of them both as Cuthbert prayed.

"O thou who art the sparrow's friend," he said, "have mercy on this world that knows not even when it sins. O holy dove, descend and roost on Godric here so that a heart may hatch in him at last. Amen."

Then he rose and placed his hand on me, nor was it any ghostly hand but warm and strong with life. "Godric, thy sins are all forgiven thee," he said. "Go now. Do good. For there's no good a man does in this world, however small, but bears sweet fruit though he may never taste of it himself."

"Father, will we meet again?" I said and grasped the hem of his coarse cloak.

"You will see Farne again," he said, "for where your treasure is, there shall your heart be too." Then before I could speak more, I fell into a sleep so deep I did not wake till well past dawn.

The boatman's foot was in my ribs.

"Rise up, man!" he said. "Or else the birds will shit you white as a Farne rock."

The sky was grey behind him. I could see his mast whip back and forth above the ledge. The man grinned down at me through crooked teeth. I asked him who he was.

"I'm Roger Mouse," he said. It was the first I ever heard the name of him who was to be my first fast friend.

How Godric met a boar and a leper and how people sought him in his cell.

I can no longer hold my water and itch in places I haven't scratched these twenty years for the clownish stiffness in my bones. It's Reginald that has to swab my bum and deems the task a means of grace. I've got an old dam's dugs. My privities hang loose as poultry from a hook. My head wags to and fro. There's times my speech comes out so thick and gobbled I'd as well to save my wind. But the jest is bitterer yet, for deep inside this wrecked and ravaged hull, there sails a young man still.

How I rage at times to smite with these same fists I scarce can clench! How I long, when woods are green, to lark and leap on shanks grown dry as sticks! Let a maid but pass my way with sport in her eye and her braid a-swinging, and I burn for her although my wick's long since burnt out and in my heart's eye see her as the elders saw Susanna at her bath—her belly pale and soft as whey, her pippins, her slender limbs and thistledown. So ever and again young Godric's dreams well up to flood old Godric's prayers, or prayers and dreams reach God in such a snarl he has to comb the tangle out, and who knows which he counts more dear.

Is he asleep, old Godric? Is he awake? Does he

himself know which? He lies there staring at a crack. He mumbles holiness. They say he first saw light in Bastard William's day, and now it's Henry Second, Becket's bane, that calls the tune from France.

They say that Godric's body's scored from when the Devil, shaped like a wild boar, fetched him down and tore him. They say he healed a leper with a kiss. They kneel there waiting for him to rise or stir while Godric mocks them in his peacock heart.

What can such whispering gawkers know of hot, foul breath, he thinks, of slobbered tusks and eyes like coals? Fierce from a thicket it sprang on him with snuffling rage, but Godric knew it for the Prince of Darkness by the golden circlet on its brow and signed it with the cross. From snout and pizzle blood spewed forth. Then, as it screamed, its maw filled up with flames till there was nothing left of it except a stench so vile that Godric swooned.

And let them say what cost the kiss I gave one rainy day on Dover Road.

I see the shape approaching still. Its clothes are patched with white and on its head a tall red hat all bent and faded pale from years of weather. *Frick-frack, frick-frack* its rattle goes, and as I climb the bank to let it pass, the very mist shrinks back to flee its touch. The mire is gullied deep, and as it nears my perch, it trips and topples to the ground. It tries to rise but flounders down again. It whimpers like a child that's being flogged. The rain is pelting hard, and flat on its belly in the muck it might well drown for all I know. So less from pity than from fear to have a murder on my soul, I go to help it to its feet. As I bend down, it turns to face me. Then I see it has no face.

I can't say if it was a man I kissed or maid or why I kissed at all. I've seen them make the sick eat broth by holding it so close the savor draws them on. Maybe misery has a savor too so if you're near enough, sick though you be with sin, your heart can't help but sup. In any case, I closed my eyes against that foul and ashen thing that once was human flesh like mine and kissed its pain. When it reached out to me, I fled till I was far enough away to puke my loathing in a ditch.

The tale they tell is of a leper cleansed. I do not know nor seek to know, for pride lies one way, rue the other. But from that time the word went forth that there was healing in my hands. *Something* was in my hands at least and rests there yet though they're all knotted now and stiff like claws. Folk come from miles to have me touch them. Could I but touch the churlishness within myself or kiss old Godric clean!

Here's how it happens when they come. They go to the monks at Durham first. "Where be the way to the hermit?" they ask. They say, "We're here to see the one as cools his holy bum in Wear come sun or snow." "To what end see him?" ask the monks, for to some I could be just as well a hanging or a calf that's got two heads. Others would sell me fowl, or have me bless some trinket, or take a snippet of my beard back home to keep off warts. And some there are who come to try me if they can.

I remember a plump maid once with apples in her cheeks and drooping lids. She'd finished telling all her fleshly sins and knelt for shriving when all at once she flung her clothes above her head and nimble as a tumbler at a fair went topsy-turvy with her bum aloft. I had my own sport then. Tune was sleeping in his jar but at my call shot forth and lunged at her. Hey nonny nonny off she went then! Nor did she stop, I'll vow, till Orkney rocks.

The monks do the sieving, as I say, and send to Godric only those deemed worthy, though I'd guess that if a gallows rat should slip a coin into their cowls, they'd send him too. And to each they give a cross of plaited straw to be his proof they've sent him. Else Reginald will drive them off.

To touch me and to feel my touch they come. To take at my hands whatever of Christ or comfort such hands have. Of their own, my hands have nothing more than any man's and less now at this tottering, lamewit age of mine when most of what I ever had is more than mostly spent. But it's as if my hands are gloves, and in them other hands than mine, and those the ones that folk appear with roods of straw to seek. It's holiness they hunger for, and if by some mad grace it's mine to give, if I've a holy hand inside my hand to touch them with, I'll touch them day and night. Sweet Christ, what other use are idle hermits for?

But then from time to time a day will dawn when suddenly my blood runs chill for thinking that what holiness I have is mine to *keep* lest, losing it, I lose the hand within my hand, my own heart's heart, my own life's life. And then I fend them off like leeches come to suck my blood. Reginald lets them in. I scowl at them. Or will not speak. Or feign some fatal ill or sleep.

Or sometimes, fierce with rage, I'll even crouch on hands and knees and shake my hair and beard into a snarl and roar at them. And sometimes even then, so great their need, they'll risk their skins by kneeling down to kiss me as they might a leper.

How Godric became Deric and sailed the
seas with Roger Mouse.

WE stood on the deck of *Saint Esprit,* myself
and Mouse. She was running free before a
wind that shook our beards, and Mouse kept his
cap pulled down about his ears. He had his arm
around my shoulder and smelled of onions. Once
in a while the sea would crest, but mostly it was
great blue hills with foam for heather. A swell
would rise and glitter in the sun, then slide and sink
into a dale. A dale would heave into a hill.

"The waves are like the years the way they melt!"
Mouse called against the wind. "Great Alfred's
arse, while yet we can, we better . . ." and then
when a gust blew off his nether words, he sang it
out for fair. "LIVE! LIVE!" he cried. And such was
Mouse. He lived and gave me lessons in the art.

He called me by the name I'd told him there at
Farne. Gudericus, I said, when asked. He said it was
too much to mouth and chopped it down to Deric.
So Deric I was to him from that day forth, nor did
he ever know of Godric. Why did I play him false
like that? I think in some way it was Cuthbert's
doing. "Do good," he bade me. He laid that holy
charge on Godric's head. But goodness was not
Godric's meat. Wealth was he after and sport and
hazard, so rather than deny the old saint's bidding,
he denied his proper name instead.

44

The boat Mouse sailed me in to Farne did not belong to him but to a Newcastle shipwright by the name of Curran that he let her from. Curran was growing dim of wit with age so it took no greater trick to gull him of his craft than the leaky tale of how we'd lost her in a squall that splintered her against the rocks. A broad-beamed, lumpish thing she was, forever thumped by every wave, but we hugged the shore with her, and she served us for a year or two of seaborne sharping. We hauled fish in her, wool and hides. We put in at fairs. What we picked up from the dullard Scots for groats we'd peddle off for pence from Yarmouth south to Ramsgate, then turn back and try to fill our purse the other way. Here or there we'd hire louts to help with loading, then keep them on as crew until the time came round to pay them for their pains. When that day dawned, we'd go ashore and in some pothouse ply them so with beer their brains were all awash, then leave them there to wonder when they waked if Mouse and Deric both were nothing but a dream.

One of these, a rogue named Colin we'd already gulled some months before, we chanced upon again inside a Portsmouth stews. Mouse had a meaty wench with painted pippins and I a wall-eyed beauty with one hand lopped off for thieving when Colin came clomping in and spotted us. It was fox and geese then down the lane, and Colin with a wicked blade and Mouse and I as bare as birth, our goosenecks flapping. Thanks be to God we somehow got away and cast off before he sniffed us out again. And so it ever was, for from the start my Mouse and I had luck.

We traded Curran's tub for shares in other craft,

each fleeter and stouter than the last, and each time
cast our cozening peddlers' nets still wider yet till
we were catching gulls and boobies as far afield as
Flanders, Denmark, France. And thus we saw the
world, did Mouse and Deric, as also did the world
see us. I won't say either side was better for the
sight, but ah, what times we had! Such romps and
routs and carefree sinning that if we'd died, un-
shriven as we were, we'd both be dangling now on
red-hot hooks in Hell. What's more we soon grew
rich as well. By the time that I was thirty-odd and
Mouse's beard already showed a sprig or two of
grey, we owned each one a moiety of the *Saint
Esprit*. She had a red sail and a high, sharp prow
and a proper crew by then that we paid proper
wages. And after a time, along with all our hides
and fish, we took to stowing pilgrims too.

From Bristol we'd haul them to Santiago de Com-
postela in seven days and back in five with the wind
our way. They'd gather on the shore all swaddled
in their shaggy robes and round felt hats, armed
with their staffs and bedding and bottles. A priest
would bless their setting forth. He even threw
another blessing in for free to cover both the *Saint
Esprit* and Mouse and me. We'd load them then.
The old and sick we'd swing aboard with ropes,
the rest would clamber on the best they could with
the freshening breeze to toss the women's skirts
on high, and how the crew would squint and crane
to see what they could see. They were Venetian
seamen mostly, as brown and spry as apes, and
naked save for clouts to hide their lechery. As the
anchor was weighed, a pilgrim often leapt upon a
barrel at the mast and with a cross clutched to his
breast would lead them in a parting psalm. "Had

not the Lord been on our side, the proudful waters would have swamped our souls," he'd chant when we put out. Months later when we moored again, "Praise to the good Christ and Virgin kind." In between they'd leave their sins with good Saint James in Spain and also, if their luck was lean, their pence and chattels in the holds of pirates.

Many times we were boarded and sacked. It happened most at night, and often they were merchant seamen like ourselves instead of true sea-robbers. They'd draw along as if for news or succor, and the next we knew, they'd have their grapples out. Sometimes they wouldn't stop at honest thieving either but would take some poor folk off to sell as slaves. At Narbonne, on the coast of France, they say a pair of Christian souls that Jesus died to save would buy a mule. Mouse and Deric they'd bind fast with ropes so there was nothing we could do but lie there gasping on the deck like fish.

Deric it was who, shame to say, from master villains such as these learned how to work some villainy of his own. Before the *Saint Esprit* put off, he'd hide himself aboard so not a pilgrim ever saw his face. Then when they were several days from shore and it was night, he'd grime his face and knot his hair and with a handful of the crew would man the cockboat that we towed astern. Then he'd have them row around amidships where the pilgrims slept, throw up a ladder, and therewith lead his men aboard with daggers clenched between their teeth and howling like a pack of fiends from Hell. "Help! Pirates! Help!" the pilgrims cried.

To dupe them further, Deric and his men would lash Mouse to the mast where he would feign to curse and threaten while they shook each pilgrim

47

like a sack until the last few groats came tumbling out. Then over the side into the cock again to split with Mouse some later time, nor any pilgrim ever saw the ruse.

Sometimes Mouse would play the pirate's part and Deric let himself be bound, and then they'd play the gammon out the same except that Mouse found pence less sweet than certain other fruit. Right there beneath the stars, in sight of God and man, I've seen him so caught up in tumbling pilgrim maids he'd clean forget the other treasure he was there to take. One time my anger grew so hot I broke my bonds and doused him with a pail of chill, grey sea. But Mouse was plunged so deep into his work, I think he never even knew.

Nonetheless our fights were few those first, far days. We loved each other, Mouse and I, and our love was born of need, for so it always is with mortal folk. God's love's all gift, for God has need of naught, but human folk love one another for the way they fill each other's emptiness. I needed Mouse for his strength and mirth and daring. Mouse needed me for my mettle and my wit. Even when the stars were mostly hid, I knew to plot a course by stars, and my parrot beak was ever keen to peck the weather's secret out. I could sniff a gale some three days off, and though we voyaged leagues away from home, I always knew when rain came trickling through my father's thatch or when the sun shone bright on Burcwen's hair.

Such was Godric's roistering at sea. His neck grew thick. His chest grew deep. His beard bloomed to a wild black bush. His wealth piled up like dung. He feared God little, men still less. He wenched and broiled. He peddled, gulled and stole. He helmed the *Saint Esprit* through many a black and windy sea. And yet. And yet. In the midst of all those stormy times there were moments too of calm when every now and then he'd set his sails again for Farne.

The holy isle would rise with pinnacles and sheer, grey cliffs all laden soft with birds. Her air was white with wings. Her silence broken only by their cries. Her winds were chill and sweet with salt.

I'd scale ashore and find the fish-shaped rock. I'd dig down with a spade so I'd be sure my trove was safe, then lay with it whatever more I had while Mouse kept watch on deck below. He'd tell the crew the lie I first told him, how I was there for penance for my sins. Thus if they chanced to spy me kneeling at my work, perhaps they even thought he told the truth. Who knows? In some way deeper than he knew, perhaps he did.

Once I thought I saw Saint Cuthbert's hare. He was crouched above me on the ledge, but when I called to him, he fled. And once I thought I saw the holy saint himself.

I was scattering pebbles on the fresh-turned soil to hide my tracks, my fingers stiff with cold, when something caused the birds to fear. A host of them rose up and filled the air. They creaked and swirled and scattered down, and it was in their midst I thought I saw him stand. His beard and cloak were white as they. He was leaning on a stick as if he'd traveled far. I thought his face was full of grief.

I reached my hands to him, but when I moved, the birds flew off, unfurled above the water like a flag. Where they had been, there was no more to see but only heather and a pile of stones. I knelt there till my beard froze stiff with tears.

How Godric journeyed home again and
Aedwen's dream.

WITH red sail ragged and a battered hull, the
Saint Esprit was in a sorry state, so we put
in at Newcastle and docked at Curran's wharf for
caulk and patching. Then Mouse and I went off our
separate ways to meet again in six months' time.
Mouse had a mind, he said, to live like royalty a
while, so he got his beard clipped short and bought
a mantle trimmed with fox and crimson boots. He
bought himself a dappled mare as well and set off
at a trot like a Norman baron.

But Godric took a plainer way. Not only had he
buried all he had on Farne, but that was Deric's
wealth, not Godric's, and even if he'd stowed it in
a wallet round his neck, he'd not have touched a
coin. For even as he felt the soil beneath his feet, it
was with Godric's feet he felt it, and Godric's was
the face he set for home, clad only in his salt-stiff
cloak and seaman's leggings.

It was as Cuthbert said. When a man leaves home,
some scrap of his heart waits there against his coming back, and it was to find that scrap again that
he tramped through all those miles of Norfolk
weather. Repentance also is a turning back, a going
home, says Reginald. But no such godly tack as
that did Godric trim to. He carried in his heart an

empty place that only those he'd left behind could fill, and to that end alone he journeyed.

But when he reached his father's house at last, it was a house without a father. Aedwen told him, and her eyes told more, no longer blue but blear and hooded. At first she did not know him for her son but like a stranger's stammered forth his name a time or two, then ran her fingers down his bearded cheeks as if to comb the puzzle out.

"Those whiskers have been twelve years blooming, Mother," he said. "The snout the same." And then she knew.

"He's dead, Godric," she said, nor was there any need to say the one she meant.

The sadness was I'd lost a father I had never fully found. It's like a tune that ends before you've heard it out. Your whole life through you search to catch the strain, and seek the face you've lost in strangers' faces.

"The grey cob kicked him in the groin while he was fettling," Aedwen said. "For weeks he spat out blood. When he made water, that was bloody too. Godric, he could not even stand but on his hands and knees would crawl out to the croft and grub. One day we found him mad with fever. He thought there was a famine. He was eating earth. He died as he was calling out your name, Godric. Six years ago come Whitsuntide we buried him. The stone is there."

Aedwen hid her face and shook. A wife has but so many tears to shed. When I took her in my arms, she was so spare I feared she'd break.

And Burcwen. How can I tell of Burcwen? It was as if the self-same sun that had dried up my mother's life had greened my sister's. What had come out like leaves along her boughs was not the loveliness that fires the flesh of such as Mouse but loveliness like shade a man finds peace and coolness in.

"You've kept your word then, Godric," Burcwen said. "You've come with treasure in your sack to build us that great house you said and make us rich."

We stood beside my father's stone where I had laid a gillyflower down.

"There lies my treasure, Burcwen," I said. "I think he never even knew."

"Perhaps he knows," she said.

"You'll be wedding some man soon," I said, "and settling in his house."

"Only the Man in the Moon," she said. "I'll have no other. I'll dangle where you hung me till he cuts me down."

"And what till then?" I asked.

"Don't be afraid, Godric," Burcwen said. "I won't chase after you a second time. The child I was is buried deep as Tom Ball buried Father," but when I turned to look at her, it was a pleading child I saw.

She did not speak her plea, for like our prayers to God, the deepest prayers we humans ask of one another speak but silence for their tongue. Yet I heard her wordless praying well, and in my heart I pondered what she asked.

What would become of a maid at sea with pirates? How could she ever understand why Deric buried wealth on Farne that would have made their fortune else? Where was a man with strength enough to lie alone on windwashed decks when such a one as she lay near with empty arms? So, like Almighty God himself, without a word, for both our sakes, I told her no.

52

I could as well have struck her. She paled and took her eyes from mine. She knelt to move my flower on the stone. And when she rose, a door had closed between us, whether to Hell or Heaven who can tell?

"Fiddledeedee," she said and laughed a small, bent laugh. "I'd never leave here in a thousand year and him with no one else to keep him." Thus she wanted me to think it was for William's sake she stayed at home, but I saw deeper. She stayed at home because once more I would not take her thence. It was her woman's pride that I had hurt and not her love that made her cleave to William.

And yet in some sad, cradling way she loved him too. Will Wagtongue was the name they called him by. As spiders spin out threads to swing on to some neighboring wall, so William spun out words to bridge him to his neighbors. Yet when they saw him floating near, they'd fly for shelter since, as spiders wrap their prey with silk, so William sought to bind folk fast with talk.

Poor soul, the more he tried to prate his loneliness away, the lonelier they left him. Nor did he ever learn to play. As most folk work to live, he lived to work, to grub, to patch and heave and gather. When all the rest had quit the fields for supper, Will Wagtongue drudged on still. I see him tread the furrows, dark and spent against the flaming sky. I hear his footfall heavy at the door. I watch as Burcwen stands to greet him.

Friend she calls him, not William or brother, as if so he will know he has at least one friend. "Friend, sup," she says. She hands a bowl to him. She squats beside him at the hearth, her hair aglow. He spoons his broth and prattles all the while. The juice runs down his chin. She wipes it clean. "Save your breath to munch with, friend," she says. Perhaps he laughs a lentil in her eye, then gently thumbs it out.

She loves him for his need of her. She loves him for his needing of her need. She loves him as a flax to staunch her wounds.

She shies a glance at sailor Godric.

"I'd never leave him in a thousand year," her silence says, and silently the sailor says Amen.

"Your father lies beneath a stone," old Aedwen mumbles, dozing at her wheel, and Godric thinks how it's a stone as well they're all beneath. The stone is need and hurt and gall and tongue-tied longing, for that's the stone that kinship always bears, yet the loss of it would press more grievous still.

After such fashion weeks went by till one day Aedwen told a dream. "Your father came to me," she said. "He's in Purgatory for his sins, though few enough they were, if you ask me. Godric, his lips were blue, his poor feet sore with kibes. It's endless ice and winter there. His moans were piteous. 'Wife,' says he, 'for Jesu's sake have mercy. Hie thee to Rome and there at Peter's tomb pray for my soul's unfettering. Then I may fly to Paradise at last that else must tarry here to freeze my cullions off. Almighty God is never deaf, they say, to pilgrims' cries.'"

Her hands were blue as Father's lips with woad from dyeing fustian for my lord, and she seized me with blue fingers round the wrists.

"Godric, you know the world," she said. "You're wise in worldly ways. You've months before you join your ship. By the paps that gave you suck and now hang flat as sandal soles, I pray you come with me to Rome. Think how my Aedlward rattles with the cold!"

And then again she hid her face and shook.

Did she truly dream her dream? Or did she only feign it as a way to flee her grief a while, to flee poor William's gabbling too and the wounding ways of me and Burcwen? Such were the sinful thoughts I had at least. But I said I'd think on it and let her know.

Why should I go to Rome? I asked myself. To free my father's soul? To please my mother? To flee, like her, the loving pains of home? To flee myself? Saint Mary, pray for us. Undo our snarl of false and true. And in the end, I said I'd go.

I asked Burcwen to come too, for this time it was not the voyage of my life that was at stake as theretofore but one that had a known and certain end. And Aedwen too would be along lest in the lonely dark we should forget that we were kin. And most of all I craved my sister's company, the ease and mirth we'd known in younger days. Even William gave us leave. He'd have to stay behind to work his croft and serve my lord, he said, but needed none to dandle him the time we were away.

But Burcwen said she would not go, and it was I her words were aimed to strike.

"Let those who will go dallying," she said. "My friend and I must husband here at home."

But by the look of her red ears and trembling lip, I knew it was herself her shaft struck deepest.

How the waters rose, and Godric spoke of
time, and the road to Rome.

ILRED was with me when old Wear went mad. Weeks of rain and melting snow had harried him to where he leaped his banks and roared through rocks and trees until my cell was all but ringed about. Then more rain lashed him on to greater fury still, and we woke at dawn to find him growling at our door.

Up to our knees in roiling surge we waded to the little church I'd hacked and hammered out of wood in honor of Our Lady years before. I was only a lad of eighty-odd and Ailred but a babe of forty, give or take, yet still it was no easy task to scramble to the roof. I got there first and hauled up Ailred afterward, who barked his shins along the way. I scraped my own arm raw against the eave. So abbot and hermit there we were, perched high like two old ravens in the wet to croak the time away till Wear grew calm. Monk Reginald was gone, praise God, so we were spared the gaggling of a goose.

Poor Ailred's cough was fierce. *Brecch! Brecch!* he'd go till tears ran down his cheeks and his bones clattered, for he was little more than bones. It was the crack of woodsmen axing oak, and if he tried to speak, it started worse, so I spoke most. Perhaps it was my thought our time was running out that put the matter in my mind, but time was what I spoke about while gentle Ailred listened. His way of listening was itself a kind of talking, though. *Say what you will,* it said. *I hear, I pardon, all.*

"Ailred, I know hours well enough," I said. "Stick a twig into the soil and watch the shadow turn. That's hours. Or take old Wear out there. Let him rise another inch or two, and either we'll grow gills or shipwreck sure. That's hours for you. It's inch by inch and hour by hour to death. It's hours gone and hours still to go. No puzzle there. A child can count it out. But what is time itself, dear friend? What is the sea where hours float? Am I daft, or is it true there's no such thing as hours past and other hours still to pass, but all of them instead are all at once and never gone? Is there no time lost that ever was? Is there no time yet to come that's not here now?"

B R E C C H ! It shook him so, I had to snatch him in my arms for fear he'd tumble off our roost. Somewhere beyond the clouds the sun was dimly up. The light and churning waters both were grey. Ailred drew his cloak about his ears. His jaws shook fierce with cold but somehow shook his message out. "We're old, we're old," he said.

"Yes!" I cried. "Perhaps it comes with growing old, these eyes that see as clear what used to be as now they see what is, or even clearer yet. Mine even see what will be too. When I was sailoring, I used to see the weather three days off, and now I sometimes see the deaths of men that still have years to live. The lad that brings me eggs, for one. He brings me pails of Wear as well, and more than eggs and pails. His name is Perkin. Surely as I see the saucy way he winks when he kneels down for blessing, I

57

see the field he'll fall on battling for a king that's not yet crowned. And this same patch of earth where I've lived now more winters through than I can count, I know how it will look when I am dust. The candles. The felled trees. The throngs of strangers in strange garb that come to pray." I closed my eyes to curtain off the sight.

"But oh, the times that were, they're worse!" I cried. "For now I'm long past mending them. Yet still they flood their banks like Wear and roar at me. Oh Ailred, is the past a sea old men can founder in before their time and drown?"

I thought of Noah on his deck with all the world awash. He had a beard like mine, an anchor for a nose and swimming eyes. "Did Noah cast a glance astern like me?" I said. "Did Noah, dreaming in his ark, still tramp the earth that forty days and nights had swallowed up? While waiting for the dove to bring some sprig of hope, did Noah travel in his mind like Godric roads still flooded fathoms deep in time? What sort of hermit can he be who has a heart that gads about the very world he's left behind for Christ?"

That little house I'd built Our Lady was my ark, and in all the watery waste of Wear that lapped us round, Ailred seemed my only sprig of hope. The rain made seaweed of our beards. The chill wind flapped our clothes like sails. Who would have guessed that he was master of the Rievaulx monks? Who would have thought that people journeyed miles to touch my hem. *Brecch! Brecch!* His hacking doubled him in half. I took his hand.

"I once saw Rome," I said. "I took my mother. We plodded many a mile. I plod them still."

And as I told him how we went, what used to be

became what was, as now again it does become what is.

It is the Lady month of May, and all is green. I mark the snowy fleece of lambs. Strawberry leaves I mark, and campion, and bluebells blue for Mary, and churchbells too that shake the high blue timbers of the sky. Cuckoos sing and throstles. The thickets buzz with bees. Barefoot lads prod sweet-breathed beasts with creamy flanks to market fairs. Oxen haul carts of stone for Norman keeps. As we near London, minstrels and chapmen jostle tinkers, quacks, and nuns. Priests with banners lead pilgrims like ourselves who tote long staffs with hooks to hang their bottles on. LIVE! LIVE! I hear Mouse cry again, for everything we see breathes bold with life. Even old Aedwen is a girl again.

Sometimes there's a stream to ford or a rain-filled pit where folk have delved for clay to mend their walls, and then I set her on my back where she rides as light as air and lighter still for all the cares she's left at home. Else, see her at my side gay as a serf let out of bond. If it's fair, we sleep by hedges. If it storms, there's monks to take us in or taverns. They're wretched places, taverns, full of whores and mice and brawls, but it's no matter. Louts thump their flasks against the board to beat a tune for some plump lass to jig to till her pippins jounce like piglings in a sack. Then see them pop the seams at last to cool their rosy snorters in the air! Old Aedwen hides her face and shakes and shakes. And pilgrim Godric goggles like an owl.

We ship from Dover. A priest thieves Aedwen's bedding on the waves, but she's too busy puking to mind much. "Poor Aedlward's in Purgatory. I'm in Hell!" she wails, and after we have docked in

France, she says for many days the earth keeps pitching still as though the world's itself a deck gone wild. And so it is.

All roads lead to Rome, they say, and ours leads us a crooked way. Great cities come and go. In Tours I catch a flux. In Lyons Aedwen twists her foot so I must load her on my back again. In Genoa a man found murdering a maid with child is cruelly punished. We watch them rope his arms and legs to four hot horses, then drive them to a rage with rods till each pulls hard a different way. But the man is young and stout and will not tear until the hangman risks their flying hooves to hack him with a sword about the joints, whereat he comes apart at last, and Aedwen swoons.

Except that there they have no end, the pains of Hell can be no sharper than the pains we suffer here, nor the Fiend himself more fiendish than a man. Oh Queen of Heaven, pray for us. Have pity on the pitiless for thy dear Son our Savior's sake.

At home the leaves are falling sere when we behold at last the seven hills of Rome.

Ailred touched my sleeve. He aimed a bony finger at the sky. The rain had nearly stopped. A ragged cloud had blown apart to bare a patch of blue no bigger than a hand. And through that rent a blessed shaft of sun shot down. It was as if a dove came winging back with olive in his mouth.

"You speak of time, Godric," Ailred said. His cough for once was gone. "Time is a storm. Times past and times to come, they heave and flow and leap their bounds like Wear. Hours are clouds that change their shapes before your eyes. A dragon fades into a maiden's scarf. A monkey's grin becomes an angry fist. But beyond time's storm and clouds there's timelessness. Godric, the Lord of Heaven changes not, and even when our view's most dark, he's there above us fair and golden as the sun." And so it is.

"God's never gone," my gentle, ailing Ailred said. "It's only men go blind."

We heard a shout and looked around. It was Reginald poling toward us on a raft. His cowl hung soaked about his ears. His gills were green. He struck our chapel with the hollow thwack of wood on wood and helped us down.

"At last you're good for something, monk," I said. For once, when he embraced me, I was almost glad.

Of Rome, a maiden, and a bear.

JACOB labored seven years to win fair Rachel for a bride, but when he woke upon the marriage bed, he found the rascal Lot had slipped her weak-eyed sister in her place. Thus was it when we came to Rome. We'd traveled months to reach the Holy City, but in its place we found unholy wreck. "Dust thou art, and unto dust thou shalt return," says God to Adam for his sins. But before we're dust, we're rot and worms and stench like wretches' bodies hung in chains. And so she was, poor Rome. Bits of flesh still clung to her like rags. Her very grin was ghoulish. She was a corpse without a shroud.

The heavy air was hard to breathe and swarmed with biting nits. Offal floated in the Tiber where poor folk drank. Dark windows stared at us like empty sockets. Rough stairs and archways beckoned us to evil courts. The reek of dung was everywhere. In tumbled shops they vended holy wares like trinkets. A coin would buy a splinter of our Savior's cross, a thimble of the Blessed Virgin's milk, or locks from good Saint Peter's pate. From crannies in the walls the painted eyes of saints gazed out at beggars, whores, and barefoot monks with candles in their hands. Knights on their way to wrest Jerusalem from the Turks stomped by in hauberks made of countless rings of steel. We saw great cardinals robed in red with perfumed kerchiefs at their lips and tresses oiled in ringlets.

Once we could have touched the Pope himself. He rode a milk-white mule with purple saddle-cloth and silver bridle. We knelt to ask his blessing, but though he glanced our way, I think it was not we he saw. His eye was sharp and vexed as though he sought some face he could not find or feared to find. When Aedwen reached her hand to him, his white mule startled and might have pitched him to the stones but for a monk who seized the rein to gentle him. We could have been a pair of Roman cats for all the Holy Father knew.

All this was the flesh that clung like tatters to the bones of Rome. The bones were sadder still. The bones were Caesar's.

Less than a score of years before, a Norman duke that held his fiefdom from the Pope had come and sacked the place. Before him, wild men from the north and hairy Huns and Lombards all had spent their fury there. The city Caesar knew lay heaped in ruins, and Aedwen gave a Roman with a crooked back a copper brooch to show us what was left.

Through groves of shattered columns he led the way, gabbling in a tongue we did not know of glories past and gone. He showed us terraces where kings had supped now gone to weeds and creeping vines. He showed us temples strewn with gods more broken than the horse-torn wretch in Genoa. He limped through marble limbs and heads and skirts and pointed out a monstrous font where once, he told by pointing at his mouth, the priests had served the gods their meat but now was turned into a stinking jakes.

I carried Aedwen on my shoulders up a hill where

goats leapt at their lecheries and dropped their berries through the fallen halls where Caesar and his lords had hatched the laws that ruled the world. Poor folk grew cabbage there and tethered dogs to poles to howl the ravens off. Roaring like a lion through his yellowed teeth and making at us with his claws as if to tear our flesh, he took us to a roofless shell as vast as all of Bishop's Lynn, and there I guessed was where in Peter's day they cast poor Christian folk to savage beasts. I wept and Aedwen too except she had no tears but only that dry grief that shook her like the wind. She had not even strength enough by then to hide her face, so I hid mine instead, thus not to seem to goggle at her pain. When I peeped out again, our guide had gone and taken off the net of cheese we'd bought to sup upon.

Why did we weep? I asked myself. We wept for all that grandeur gone. We wept for martyrs cruelly slain. We wept for Christ, who suffered death upon a tree and suffers still to see our suffering. But more than anything, I think, we wept for us, and so it ever is with tears. Whatever be their outward cause, within the chancel of the heart it's we ourselves for whom they finally fall.

We'd tramped so far from home and found so little for our pains. We'd started forth so full of hope and gaiety who now sat sore of foot among the rubble of those brutish lists. Still darker yet, we'd come to pray to God for mercy on my father's soul, and lo, save only for those heaps of marble limbs and heads, we found no God in Rome. If God was there, then like the Pope the eyes he cast on us were blind.

And yet to pray we'd come and pray we did. We climbed Saint Peter's stairs upon our knees and stopped at each to plead for Aedlward. Inside, the church was full of smoke. Gold vessels gleamed. Holy paintings glowed upon the walls as priests moved by with tapers. Some were pilgrims like ourselves. Some, I think, were only there for shelter. A crone so old she looked like Caesar's nurse sat selling badges crossed with Peter's keys to stitch upon our cloaks. A lass so young the tender breasts she bared were scarcely more than pigeon eggs made clear enough the wares she sold although she spoke no word I understood. A silk-capped cardinal with pretty boys in cowls to serve him sang mass at the high altar like a love-sick maid, and from his hands we took the blood and flesh of Christ. A trapped bird beat his wings above.

Aedwen and I lay flat upon the paving-stones where underneath they say the bones of Peter rest.

"Holy Jesu, gentle Lord," I prayed, "have pity, for thy friend the fisherman's sake, on my poor father. His great ears were always cold in life, and now in Purgatory's thrall they're like to freeze. Cast down thy nets and fish him from the icy depths. Forgive him all he ever did or left undone that was not pleasing in thy sight. Oh haul him up that he may sing thy praise in Paradise!"

I breathed my words into the chill, grey stone, but the lips of him I prayed to, like the stones themselves, were still. When you butt the bottom of the sea, there is no farther you can fall.

Now shift your gaze.

See Godric and his mother trudging home.

Somewhere along the way they come upon a grove of fig trees on a hill. They pluck some fruit and sit them down to sup. The fruit is sweet, and sweet and warm the sun. Aedwen leans against a

twisted trunk and buzzes off to slumber like a bee.
Godric only sits and stares. He's empty as a drum
inside his skin, but there's a kind of peace in emptiness. No fear or hope awakes in him. He thinks no
thoughts. He hardly breathes. His eyes alone are
live.

Slowly then, before he knows a name for it or
cares, a shape heaves into view among the farther
trees. It's dark and shaggy with a clumsy gait. It
halts to sniff the air. It turns and rolls its head about
and gapes, then raises up and plants among the
leaves its snout and two great paws. And only then
does Godric see it for a bear.

With snuffling greed it gobbles up the fruit, then
claws another branch for more until the juice runs
dripping from its chops. The sod beneath is thick
with fallen figs, and plumping down on all four
pads again, it roots and wallows in them like a sot.
At last, with swollen paunch, it lumbers off a pace
or two, turns tail and there, in Godric's view, voids
all that sweetness out its hinder part. Then Godric
turns to see if Aedwen saw and finds a maiden at
her side.

How can an old man sing a young man's song
but croakingly? What colors can he find in words
to limn a face so fresh it blooms within him still?
Say flaxen hair? Say eyes of periwinkle blue? Say
lily brow and throat, and cheeks the tender rose
of shells? Say, rather, only wondrous fair and
seemly, then say no more lest old man's wind should
puff the dream away. She smiled at me. She said
her name was Gillian.

"You are the bear, dear heart," she said. "The figs
are Christ's sweet grace and charity. You've supped
on him for years and years, then spewed him out

your nether end in lust and lies and thievery. Thus by your sinning, like the loathly bear, you turn to dung the precious fruit that else would make you whole. Repent and mend your ways, I pray, lest all be lost."

"Oh Gillian, stay and be my strength!" I cried, but before my lips were closed, she'd gone, and there was Aedwen staring at me like an owl.

"Did you see her, Mother, where she went?" I cried. "The maid that came and spoke with me?"

"I saw no maid. Lie down," she said. "These Romish figs have turned your Saxon brain."

*Of a band of pilgrims and a parting in
a wood.*

WE joined with other pilgrims on the journey
home. They came from London town, and
how it warmed the heart to hear our native tongue
again! An onion is an onion still no matter how
you call it. A man's a man, a tree's a tree, and God
is God, but when a Norman names them or a Dane
or Roman, there's something lost. The ear takes
comfort from the sounds of home, and the out-
landish speech of foreign folk makes all the world
seem strange.

There was Richard the baker and Peg his wife.
Peg was a sparrow with a peck so sharp there was
no proof against it. All was amiss, to hear her chirp,
and she was ever chirping. If the sun was warm, she
said it stewed her brains. If a cool breeze blew, she
squawked of chilblains. The Holy Ghost himself
she would have found too holy had he come and
perched by her, I think, and Richard was her fa-
vorite prey. Whatever roughness of the road or turn
of weather vexed her, Richard was the one she
blamed.

"That I should live to see this day!" she'd cry. "I
break my toes on heathen ruts, and see my wedded
husband shake with mirth!"

Richard was a waddling goose whose feet flung

sideways when he tramped. It's true he laughed too much, but Peg had pecked and pecked till he was silly in the head. He laughed the way geese gaggle, less from mirth than brainless barnyard rote. Wedded to Peg myself, I would have wept. I think his laughter was but Richard's way of tears.

Ralph Bodo was a mason with many tales to tell of lofty lords he'd met while trimming stones for lordly keeps and towers. He said the Conqueror himself once came upon him pissing near a trough and spoke a kingly jest. "Norman sand and Saxon stale make mighty mortar," William said, and Ralph never tired saying it again. His finger ends were flat and frayed, and a wayward mallet cost him half a thumb.

Then there was Maud. Maud claimed she was the widow of a knight and wore a mantle cuffed with squirrel to prove it. She never dipped her nippers in the pot but used an ivory spoon. Her nose she hoisted high as if the whiff of common folk might clog it up, but Maud the Bawd was how Peg dubbed her to her back and swore she'd seen her creep on Richard in the night to whisper lewdness in his ear.

John Cherryman was the ancient priest who herded us. Three sons had fallen in his sight at Senlac, and he wore a chain about his neck for each. Even the smallest noises frightened him. Let a crow but caw or some branch creak, and his eyes would spin like wheels. His groaning in the night was such that one time Ralph the Mason heaved a stick that caught him on the snout, and poor priest Cherryman bled cherry red till dawn.

And sometimes Gillian came. I was kneeling at a pond to quaff when suddenly the water's glass showed forth her face behind me. There were green frogs in the reeds that croaked their froggish grief to see the summer pass, but when she spoke, they held their tongues from courtesy.

"Such drink will leave you thirsting yet," she said. "Take heed."

"Are you a pilgrim, Gillian, like myself?" I asked. "You come and go like wind."

"To puff you on a truer course," she said. Her laughter was a silver bell. "Your hull is thick with barnacles. There's mice that nibble at your shrouds. Rocks wait ahead the way you drift. Christ was a sailor too in Galilee. Hand him your helm."

"I prayed to him in Rome," I said. "It was like calling down an empty well."

Said Gillian, "Could it be it's he instead that's calling you?"

I said, "But silence has no voice to call."

"The voice of silence calls, 'Be still and hear,' poor dunce," she said. "The empty well within your heart calls too. It says, 'Be full.' "

"Oh Gillian, I thirst, I thirst," I said.

"Then drink your fill, old bear!" she cried, and dowsed my head so deep into the pond that when I dredged it up again, my beard was green with weeds, and she was gone.

Often too she came at dusk. After they'd supped, our pilgrim band would spread their cloaks to rest. Old Cherryman would close his eyes to curtain off the field at Senlac. Sparrow Peg would twit and peck till Richard gaggled off to sleep and mason Ralph clapped hands to ears like trowels. The lady Maud would bed a pace or two apart lest folk pass by and take her for a churl like us. Aedwen was always first to sleep so she might ferret through her dreams to find if Aedlward was warm again.

Then I'd see Gillian moving through them like a breeze through trees, so soft as scarce to stir a leaf. She'd bear a basin in her arms to wash my feet of dust and weariness, then dry them with her skirt. If I should ever seek to speak, she'd lay a finger to her lips. Once Aedwen woke and looked at her, but I think she fancied she was dreaming still of Paradise, for soon again she dozed.

Later, when the nights grew chill, I dreamed that I was by the hearth at home, but when I woke, I found the warmth was Gillian. A man is rarely master of his flesh beside a slender maid beneath his cloak, but she was sleeping there so chaste and still I could have been a marble lord beside a marble lady on a tomb, nor did a single fleshly thought arise to fret me as I watched the starlight in her hair.

I saw her last upon the Dover road, where after many years I kissed the leper. There was a sharp wind blowing off the sea, and I'd climbed the bank for firewood. I found her waiting by a tree. There was no color in her cheeks. Her brow was shadowed. She said she'd come to bring me news.

"Here is the sight I saw," she said. "A man was standing to his knees in snow. More snow was falling. All about, the earth was white. There was no shelter anywhere. He held his bare hands tucked beneath his arms and stood there jigging up and down. Sometimes, for comfort, he would whistle through his teeth. Sometimes he cried out piteously with no one but the stinging flakes to hear. His clothes were thin and poor. The cold was cruel."

Gillian seemed to feel the cold herself. She trembled as she spoke and drew her mantle close.

"Even as I watched," she said, "it happened thus. Down from above a slender ladder came, the same as Jacob dreamed of with his head upon a stone. Its upper part was lost in blowing snow. Its lower hung a clothier's yard or two above his head. Again and again he hopped for it, yet each time tumbled back into the drifts. But then at last his fingers hooked the nether rung, and after dangling there awhile, he gave a tug and heaved himself aloft. I still can see the way he clung. His feet were blue. The harsh wind lashed the rags about his shanks. The hands he started climbing with were seamed with soil from years of honest grubbing."

"And what of his ears, Gillian? Tell me of the ears he wore!" I cried.

"They stood out from his head like handles on a pot," she said, and then, as in that monstrous shell at Rome, I wept. But this time they were tears of hope and thankfulness.

"Where is he now?" I said. My voice was broken.

"Leg over leg he mounts to where he'll wait your coming, child, for even in Paradise there is no peace at last till all we love find peace as well. Pray, fail him not," she said.

"Oh Gillian, be my guide!" I cried. "The waves are vast, and I am far from port!"

Said she, "Would that I might, but Gillian has her own long way to wend. We all are pilgrims on this earth. My time has come to say farewell."

Once more I cried. "Stay, Gillian! Stay for Jesu's sake!"

"For Jesu's sake and thine, I go," she said. "Dear heart, farewell," and when I reached to take her in my arms, it was the tree I clasped, and pressed my cheek against the rough, grey bark.

"What keeps you, Godric?" Aedwen called me from the road below. "Without some wood to burn, we'll surely freeze!"

I found some faggots in the end, and with a flint we fired them. Old Cherryman and Peg and Maud and Aedwen. Ralph the mason with his half a thumb and fat goose Richard. They stood there in a ring around the blaze on Dover road, and I stood with them too. But though the flames leapt hot and high, there's part of me that to this day has never thawed.

Of Falkes de Granvill.

WHEN we reached home at last with winter on its way, I found a messenger from Mouse had come and gone. His message was the *Saint Esprit* lay still unpatched in Curran's slip at Newcastle. They wouldn't have her tight again till spring, and Mouse would meet me then. Burcwen told me.

"Who's Deric?" she said. "The man kept saying Deric this and Deric that. When I vowed I'd never heard of him, he scratched his head and gaped."

I told her sailors were an addled lot from beer and tossing. I told her we had a crewman by the name of Deric, and the messenger had got us mixed. "Deric and Godric ring alike," I said, "but there, thank God, the likeness ends. Deric's a lout that gives himself to lust and lies and thievery. The world would be a fairer place with Deric dead. And so he'll surely be, and soon, if Heaven's just."

"I see you've learned great charity in Rome," said Burcwen.

I'd hoped our months apart would heal her bitterness. It was not so. William was the stick she sought to drub me with. What sport they'd had, her friend and she! she cried. Even their toil was sport, she said. William would guide the heavy plow down ridge and furrow by its stilts while plodding next him with a goad, she'd drive the ox, and all the time they'd sing and jest.

"Was it not so, my friend?" she'd say to William as if all other friends were false. She'd hold his hand in hers. She'd lean her head against his shoulder. Her tenderness was William's meat and drink, for William's tenderness for her was true, nor did he ever guess that hers for him, though true in part, was partly feigned to turn my envy green.

I tried to tell her of the sights we'd seen—the Holy Father on his mule, the broken gods, the bear among the figs—but as I spoke, she'd move about and hum as if to say no sights that she and William had not seen were worth the seeing. Only of Gillian I said nothing. I did not even speak her name lest Burcwen should make light of her or rattle turnips in a pot while I spoke of how we parted in the wood. My whole life long I've never told a soul of Gillian for fear to breathe her forth into the world with words would be to risk the world's wind blowing her away.

Thus weeks passed by of hidden strife between myself and Burcwen. Each longed to be the other's friend, but pride and hurt kept her from me, and fear, I think, kept me from her. I feared the wrong I'd do poor William by wooing off the only friend he had. I feared if she and I grew close again, our parting would be harder still in spring. And most of all I feared my loneliness might make me seek to draw to her too close. I feared myself. And such was home.

I had no heart to stay and neither heart to leave nor any place to go. And then, by luck or lack of luck, a door to flee through opened up. One Falkes de Granvill came to tarry with my lord a while.

He was another Norfolk lord, but rich and mightier yet.

I came upon them in the church one morning after mass. My lord was full of cheer and with a gloved hand clapped me on the back and made me known to Falkes.

"Here's freeman Godric, my liege," he said. "Take note of him. It's plain to see he's no great beauty, but behind those Saxon whiskers lurks a rogue to reckon with. He's sailed the seven seas, he says. He's peddled wares from here to where the world drops off. He's master of a ship that ferries pilgrims to and fro like salted herrings. He's been to Rome. What say you, Godric? Kiss the hand of one who, if your press your suit, might prosper you yet more."

The hand I kissed was heavy as a bishop's with rings of gold and colored stones. My lord de Granvill was himself a new-laid egg. Not a single hair grew on his head and not a whisker on his chin. His brows were painted on with ochre.

I said, "God prosper you, your worship. For me, I have no suit to press nor look for alms from any man." I saw I pleased him with the speech I'd hewn out rough to please. His glance was weasel-sharp. He spoke our tongue but with a Norman bite.

He said, "My steward's dead, poor wretch. Saint Andrew's fire took him. My manor wants an eye to see my franchise duly granted, my greenwood free of poaching rogues, and all my tillage justly done. It wants a hand to gather taxes, rents and scutage. My villeins want a foot to kick them sore whenever they stray or nip each other at the trough. Think you the master of a ship can master clods that walk like men and even grunt a human word or two but have plowed and delved and eaten earth so long they're less of flesh than earth themselves?"

"Shape earth upon a wheel," I said, "and earth's a pot, your honor. Tread it down hard beneath your feet, and it's a floor. What's a stout wall," I said, "but earth heaped high? The earth can serve you well enough, my lord. You only need to work it to your will."

"The man speaks fair," de Granvill said, but it would have fitted better if he'd said "speaks foul," for foul it was to speak not what I truly thought but what I thought he truly wished to hear.

Shape on a wheel, like earth, poor folk Christ shed his precious blood to save? Tread down, like earth, poor souls like Aedlward who grubbed and grubbed until they grubbed for him a grubber's earthy grave at last? But Falkes de Granvill was a gate to flee my pain. For passage through, I would have licked his spittle with my tongue.

He took me by the beard and pulled me close enough to smell the blessed sacrament upon his lips and count the flakes of ochre on his brow.

He said, "Master Godric, by Christ's eyes, if ever I catch you cozening me, I'll have you flayed. But if you play me true, you'll find my hand as generous as my pate is bare. How say you then?"

My answer was to crook my knee and swear true fealty. De Granvill said we'd leave in three days' time. As steward, he said, I'd have a steed. He said to trim my beard and eat no onions, for my breath was foul. That done, I could have been a stick of wood for all he marked me. He tied an ermine bonnet underneath his chin, then called my lord to heel, and through the churchyard, past my father's stone, left footprints in the newly fallen snow.

On the third day at sun-up, we were set to go,

and what a gaudy sight it was! Baron Falkes was bound from one of his great castles to the next, and you'd have thought he carried with him all except the stones themselves. One sumpter horse was all but lost beneath his bed piled high with sheets, rugs, furs and mattresses. Another hauled his robes and clothes alone. There was a four-legged kitchen hung with cauldrons, pans, and all the clanking gear of cookery while, close behind, a chapel with a mane and tail broke wind. Candlesticks it bore and hangings stitched in wool and silk with holy pictures and, across its rump, an ivory Jesu on a wooden cross. Two-wheeled carts were heaped with wines and armor. Servants mounted mules.

De Granvill sat a crop-tailed bay up front that pawed the frost and spun. The beast was hot to run, but his master made no move to cool him. Instead, he held him in so tight, his spume was flecked with crimson from the bit. The chaplain and the chamberlain rode near, and nearer yet the falconer who bore a belled and hooded merlin on his wrist. Aedwen and William came to wave farewell. Aedwen tossed me up a sack with two fresh loaves and cheese within. William kissed my hand as if I was a lord. When I asked where Burcwen was, he toed the ground and mumbled in his beard.

At last a maid came riding on a palfrey draped in silk with serving women trotting at her side. By the stormy frown de Granvill gave, I knew she was the one we waited for. Her face was pale and freckled and her brows so fair I thought at first she lacked them like her lord. Twelve or thirteen winters were the most she could have shivered through, and thus I took her for the baron's child. Later, I found she was his high-born Saxon wife, the lady Hedwic.

The baron spurred his bay so sharp it nearly pitched his bonnet off with leaping forward, and then just as the sun had cleared the tallest oaks, the whole great train of men and beasts and chattels started forth.

William wept and Aedwen shook to watch me go, but Burcwen never came. She doubtless thought her staying off would wound me worse than any words she might have found to speak. And so it did.

How Godric served a noble lord.

REGINALD wakes me from a dream of Farne. He thinks me dead at last and holds a feather to my lips. The tickling fetches me away from where I roam that holy isle whose cliffs are white with feathers of their own. I'd dreamed I watched a rock where seals were gathered in the mist. Their snouts were pointed at the sky to tongue their plaintive, whiskered song. The plaint I hear instead is Reginald's.

"He's gone! He's gone!" he cries. "The holy hermit's breathed his last."

"I'll breathe a plague on you," I say. "I'll thrust your feather down your throat to stop your mewing."

"Praise God, you live!" cries Reginald.

I say, "Praise God, I'll someday see the last of you and die."

He's here to write his book. He lays his parchment on a stone and dips his quill. "Long ago you served a noble lord," he says. "Pray tell of that. If you'd stayed on, you could have risen to a lord yourself. Instead, you gave it up and left for love of Christ. Is that not so, Father?"

"Reach me my cup," I say, and when he stoops for it, I catch him with my foot. He smiles a crooked, moist-eyed smile that makes me flush for shame. I growl and turn my back but suffer him.

I say, "For love of Christ, I'll tell you what you ask. Perhaps you'll love to hear. Perhaps you won't. When I have done, we'll see. In the meanwhile, dowse your quill in honey, for the truth's a bitter brew."

Like Jacob's, my pillow is a stone, and when I raise myself to prop my back on it, my iron vest nips deep into my flesh. The nip's to chasten me and keep me mindful of the crueler nips our Savior bore for us upon the cross, but now it only goads the beast in me. Time and again, with rage, I hurl my back against the stone to punish stone and back as well until my irons clank like hammers on a forge. My beard is stuck with straws from sleeping. My eyes are wild. I clank my flesh so raw I roar with pain. Poor Reginald's aghast and blocks his ears.

When at last my fit is done, I lie there gasping. My cheeks that age has hollowed out are filled with shade. Deep within their sockets, my eyes are shut. My great snout towers. I feel a cool hand on my brow and just for a moment think it might be hers whom all these years I've only seen in dreams. I open my eyes to see it's only Reginald, and tears run down my face against my will. I cannot hold my blubbering back. Sweet lord, have mercy on old men who've turned to helpless babes again in every way except they loathe their helplessness.

I forget why Reginald has come until he speaks. "You were going to tell me of the noble lord, Father," he says. For once I'm glad to think of Falkes de Granvill as a thought less grievous than the one I set aside to speak of him.

"The noble motto of that noble lord was this," I say, "and often have I heard it on his lips. 'Baseborn folk, like willows, sprout better for being cropped.' Such was the noble law he ruled his manor by. My task, as steward, was to see it carried out.

"With notches on a stick I kept account of lands and fiefs. I had a clerk to list the acres each man tilled and in what crops. I tallied up the rents and days of service each man owed, the fines. I tramped through barnyards to make sure the beasts were duly kept and fattened. Each night I met with cook and pantler to oversee the food brought in to serve my lord at table on the following day. So many fowl, so many joints, so many loaves and quarts of beer. The beef was sliced up in my sight and counted out lest, while we slept, some hungry rogue would thieve a bit.

"Once when sixteen eggs were missing, it fell to me to sniff the robber out, and later it was I again who sat as judge in manor court and handed down the noble justice of my lord. The wretch was ordered flogged and hanged. His wife was there, her belly great with child. She seized his feet and tried to swing from them to cut his suffering short. 'The rope's not stout enough for three,' de Granvill said and bade the hangman pull her down."

It's Reginald's turn to weep. "The law's the law," he says, "but was there no mercy in the baron's heart to temper it?"

"The willow sprouts from being cropped," I say. "I saw the cropping duly done."

"Had he no love in him? No tenderness?" Reginald's face is not a face for showing grief. His mouth's instead for godly, monkish smiles.

I say, "He loved the land. What Norman doesn't? For land is might, and might is wealth, and wealth is swords and Norman keeps to guard the land. He loved the hunt as well. You should have seen him at it."

"Ah, then there was some good in him," says Reginald. He can't allow that any man be wholly bad, for where's God's image if we're rotten to the core? Maybe he's right. Maybe in the greenwood, giving chase, some all but snuffed-out spark of God flamed up in Falkes.

He loved his dogs at least, his sweet-tongued hounds and silken brachets. He loved his mounts. His quarry too I think he even honored in his way —the fallow deer, the harts, the boars with tusks so sharp I've seen them slit a man from knee to breast with one great stroke. Many a time I've watched his courtly gallop through the trees, his bald head glittering like a helm, his richest garments on his back, as if he rode to bring a royal prince to bay. He'd raise to his lips his ivory horn, the oliphant, and blow a string of high-pitched notes to mind his huntsmen to unleash the hounds. I've seen him with an arrow to the depth of one hand slantwise in his flesh yet smile as if it was no price too high to see a noble, antlered head brought low.

"And his lady wife?" says Reginald. "He surely must have loved her too."

"He loved the hope of sons. He had no heir," I said. "She was only a child herself, but they say that every night and morn he'd grimly lie with her that she might bring forth children though behind his back they jested that a beard was not the only part of manhood that he lacked. I know only that her pale young face grew paler yet each time she laid her eyes on him. The lady Hedwic's griefs were many, and once she spoke to me of them."

"If it please you, the lady's name again?" says Reginald. His quill is poised. If God had come to Reginald and not to Moses in the burning bush, he would have asked him how to spell the great I AM so he'd be sure he had it right.

"Hedwic," I said. "A Saxon name like Godric, monk, though what it means I neither know nor care. But what she meant was plain enough. We were feasting side by side at the high table in my lord's great hall. Candles set on spikes lit up the walls. The hearth was blazing. All around us lords and ladies stuffed like swine while servants staggered under loads of meat to stuff them more. Minstrels played on pipes and lutes, and dogs at war for scraps made music of their own beneath the board. My lord had left his massive chair. His lady wife and I were by ourselves there on the bench. She touched my sleeve.

"Look at the floor, Godric," she said in her thin child's voice. I looked and saw it freshly strewn with rushes.

She said, "My lord this morning bade me tell the chamberlain to have them sweeten it with herbs against the feast, and so I did. They scattered lavender and mint and winter savory all about till now it's fit for royal feet. And pennyroyal too, that makes me think. I doubt if there's a sweeter floor in all of Christendom. But, Godric, do you know what's underneath?"

I shook my head. I thought the wine had made her giddy the way she closed her eyes and shivered. But when she opened them again, I saw that wine was not the cause. If we'd met as simply man and child, I'd have taken her upon my knee and tried to lullaby the pain away.

"What's underneath is turds of dogs and grease and spit and bits of bone," she said. "The part you see is fair and fresh. The part you do not see is foul. Do you know what it reminds me of, this floor?"

Again I shook my head though I had guessed her meaning well enough.

"My life," she said, and hid her face.

I can't forget the bitter tale she whispered then. The lustless lust for heirs that had the baron harshly mounting her before she'd even started in to bleed as women do. The way he decked her out in silk and precious stones yet treated her like dung. The way he mocked her father for a thick-skulled Saxon dunce for giving twice the dower he'd have settled on. Her loneliness. Her shame. Her sin. "For surely it's a mortal sin," she said, "to hate him as I do and hate myself for hating him. I'd shake with fear of Hell except I think I'm there already as the Devil's bride. Godric, do you know the very food we eat is hellish?"

"My lady must be calm," I said, but she was past such soothing.

"They say it's venison," she said. "I know it's not. His huntsmen take the deer they slay and line their pockets with the coins they sell them for. They steal the poor folk's sheep and once they're flayed and stripped pass them for deer instead. Right now my belly's full of meat some poor man starves for want of. Oh Godric, are we damned for fattening on another's sin and never breathing out a word to set it right?"

"Poor child," says Reginald, "yet wiser than a child to cut sin up so fine."

"Say rather it was Godric that she cut," I say, "and cut him to the bone, poor child, though she never

85

meant me harm. I saw that it was truly I that fattened on De Granvill's baseness."

What a net of sin I'd gotten tangled in. For weeks, unknowingly, I'd eaten food from the mouths of folk with scarcely food enough to keep alive, and now I knew, I no more dared to tell my lord than Hedwic did. Either he would have me flayed for speaking false or have his huntsmen hanged for thievery, and either way he'd find some means of adding to his lady's woes. So part from fear for me and part from charity for them, I held my tongue. My silence made me party to their sin as well. Nor was that all, for every day I cropped to make de Granvill's willows sprout, my other guilt grew heavier with my purse. Working for him, I worked my own damnation, aided his, and made the Hell of those I cropped more hellish still. And Hedwic's too.

She looked to me, her only friend, for help, and I had none to give except for words. "Hold fast to Christ," I said, and she to me, "In Hell, you are the only Christ I have," but like Our Lord's upon the cross, my hands were nailed. I also feared that seeing us together overmuch, de Granvill would be harsh with her for bringing shame upon his rank. So for love of her I wounded her by keeping from her sight, and thus my love stung both of us like hate.

At last I formed a plan. One winter's eve I sought the baron in his chamber and begged a word with him. He was holding a plate of burnished silver on his knees so he could see to paint his brows with ochre from a pot. I suppose he meant, for vanity, to make himself more fair before he went in to his wife. He wore a lambskin cap against the cold. I'd

86

thought my words out well and spoke them carefully. The chief thing was to name no names.

The rumor was, I said, that certain men were stealing villeins' sheep. Knowing him to be a just and Christian lord, I said, I knew he'd want to stop such sport. A general word some night from the high table would be enough to frighten them. Then God would bless him, and the poor would bless him too and serve him all the better for his charity.

I waited full of dread to hear what he would say. If my counsels rubbed him sore, there was no telling where his wrath might strike. He might press me to tell him who the robbers were and then make bloody work of them. Or I might be the one he'd bloody with the knout the way I've seen him have the flesh flogged off men's backs till you could count their slippery ribs beneath. Or might he guess that Hedwic was the one whose tender heart had made her broach the matter to me first? Such awesome risks as these I ran, and ran them most, I think, for Aedlward's sake and all poor folk whose paltry sheep are all the meat they have.

The noble lord thrust his brush back in the pot and scowled. A cup of wine stood by him, and he took a draught, but even as he drank, he kept his eyes on mine. Then he wiped his lips, tossed back his head, and laughed so loud the stone walls cast his laughter back at him.

"Poor dolts!" he cried. "You could steal their women right beneath them in the act. They'd never know. Maybe a ewe or two the less will screw their wits a turn or two the more."

Again he roared with mirth and wine, and only when he'd finished did I try to speak again. But this time his roar was of another sort. He struck the board so hard his winecup danced. "Go hawk your wares some other place, peddler Godric!" he cried, and I withdrew before he cast me out.

Later that night I left his hall for good. I had sins enough already on my head. To stay could only load me down with more. So off I stole in moonless dark. As I passed beneath the chamber where I knew the lady Hedwic lay, I heard her weeping like a child. And thus my very flight from sin was sin itself, to take from her the only hope she had.

When I end my tale I mark that Reginald has gone and know the reason why. Sometimes when I think I'm speaking words that all can hear, it's only in my head I speak. My jaw flaps shut and open like a windy door, but not a sound comes forth. So why should Reginald stay to watch my noiseless gabbling? Indeed, why should he come at all to ask me questions when he's sure already of the truth? He's sure that Falkes de Granvill, as a noble lord, was ever noble. He's sure that Godric never would have left save for the love of Christ. Thus like a child that fashions poppets out of muck, a monk makes saints of flesh and blood.

Reginald is gathering sticks beside the Wear. I am alone. I close my eyes and pray the current of some dream will drift me back to hear again the seals' sweet song.

Of the rescue of a king and a cruel farewell.

Ah Mouse! How good it was to meet with you that spring! How good to feel the sea beneath my feet again instead of Norman stone even though the feet were Deric's that I stood upon!

"By good Saint Peter's pizzle!" you said. "You look as frazzled as a monk I know who tupped his way through a whole house of nuns beginning with the abbess."

At first I hardly knew you for your patch. A tavern brawl, you said. But one eye left, you said, was all it took to spot a plump-pursed pilgrim or a maid who'd do it free.

"And what of you, old Deric mine?" you asked. "How many have you laid with since the last we met?"

"Not even one," I said. I lied, for there was one, but I'd have sooner died than speak of her. I dared not tell you how she chastely crept beneath my cloak that night. I could not name to you my wonder as I watched her face turned marble by the moon for fear you'd bare your crooked teeth in mirth. It's less the words they say than those they leave unsaid that split old friends apart.

Yet say for sure we had our sport still, you and I, even that last year we sailed as mates. We drank our pints. We sang our songs. On windless nights we'd lie out on the decks of *Saint Esprit* and live again through many times we'd had. We spoke of how a great wave washed me overboard, and if you'd not leaped in and seized me by the beard, my bones would be a cage for fishes now. We spoke of loutish Colin chasing us with murder in his eye through Portsmouth streets. I brought to mind the day we drank ourselves so daft with beer we thought that if we spread our arms and flapped, we'd fly like birds—then flapped into a ditch. And yet there was a sadness too that hid in all we said.

When friends speak overmuch of times gone by, often it's because they sense their present time is turning them from friends to strangers. Long before the moment came to say goodbye, I think, we said goodbye in other words and ways and silences. Then when the moment came for it at last, we didn't say it as it should be said by friends. So now at last, dear Mouse, with many, many years between: goodbye.

We'd sailed the farthest that we ever had with a band of pilgrims bound to see the holiest city of them all, Jerusalem. Mouse had urged we fall on them like pirates on the way, but I said no. To send them robbed and penniless to worship at the tomb of Christ seemed even to Deric sin too deep. Mouse swore and grumbled, but he let me have my will. The winds of spring were fair, and we made good time to Arsuf, where we put in at the port for drink. It was a fateful day.

A great battle had been newly fought between the Frankish knights and heathen Turks. The Franks were far outnumbered, and the nearby fields of Ramleh were as thick with corpses as de Granvill's floor with herbs. Arsuf was in a state of terror and misrule. Women and children flew about like birds before a gale. Strong men made haste to flee, their camels loaded down with all they owned. The Turks had left a Christian church in flames, and smoke had turned the daylit streets to dusk. Looters broke the walls of shops and scattered what they could not carry off. Thus fruit and meat and costly wares were trampled underfoot.

Infidels in colored robes and yards of cloth wound round their heads set up a fearful keening in the square. A madman in a tower screamed some gibberish down that set the folk below to groveling with their noses in the dust. Mouse and I had each a great skin filled with water on our backs and were just about to load them in the cockboat when we heard a voice behind us cry, "God wills it!" in a voice of brass. We turned to see a sight that still is fresh.

A tall knight sat astride a charger deep of chest and richly decked with plaques of silver, plaited mane, and leather fringe. He wore a scarlet mantle with a coronet of gold upon his brow. His beard and hair were fair and overflowed his breast. His face was stern and battle-stained. One arm was wrapped with cloth the blood seeped through.

"God wills you take me on your craft!" he cried. "Jaffa is in peril, Jerusalem's port. If I'm not there, it falls for sure. Jerusalem then falls next and all our work undone. The ungodly Turk will foul the places sacred to Our Lord. I alone am left alive by God's good grace to save this day. I am de Bouillon's brother. Baldwin is my name. Under Christ, I am Jerusalem's king."

"Then haste to stow your royal bum aboard!" cried Mouse, and so he did. If horses weep, his charger wept with nostrils flared and piercing wail to watch us row his master to the *Saint Esprit,* where huddled pilgrims crouched in fear of death.

How far away that time, and yet how near. I see the king stand bleeding at the mast. I watch the sail fill up with wind. I hear gulls cry. And through a pair of ragged Saxon rogues, God's will is done.

The harbor of Jaffa is ringed around with clumsy Turkish craft, but the *Saint Esprit* slips through them like an eel. King Baldwin speaks no further word to Mouse and me but does a courtly deed. He draws his sword and holds the jeweled hilt to his lips. Its shape is like the cross of Christ. He kisses it and motions us to kneel. He takes it then and touches each of us upon the brow. Back on our feet again, he clasps us in his arms like brothers, and when we come apart our cheeks as well as his are wet with royal tears.

We row him into shore. The city throbs with life again to have its kingly heart back beating in its breast. It holds the Turks at bay till fresh troops come. Jerusalem is saved.

And so God willed. I cannot think he willed what happened next, and yet who knows? Sin and grace go hand in hand, they say, and the time had come for sin to take its turn. The pilgrims all had paid us dear to sail them there, and they were hot to set their feet at last on holy soil. Then Mouse brewed up a cunning scheme.

He told them that the price they'd paid had been to bring them safe to anchor here, and anchored now and safe they duly were. Thus was our bargain kept. But between our anchorage and shore, he said, a watery way was still to go. Nor was it meet that we should row them in for nought. So for one fur-

ther service, it was only just there be one further
fee to pay, and the sum he named was half what
they'd already paid to carry them across the whole
vast sea. Unless they'd rather swim ashore, he said.
If so, they'd better arm themselves with steel, for
May, he warned, was when sea-serpents hungered
most for Christian flesh. The pilgrims wept and
shook their fists and prayed. Then I took Mouse
aside.

Praise God, I have not kept in mind the words
we spoke. I chided him for dealing thus with poor
and godly folk when the touch of Baldwin's
sword was fresh still on our brows. I vowed I'd have
no part in it. I said we'd grown already fat enough
on pilfering, and if he ravened yet for more, I'd let
him wolf my share.

Mouse swore that I had played him false. He told
me just because I hadn't tupped a maid for all those
months, I thought I was some kind of gelded saint.
He mocked and cursed at me. He blessed the day
he'd lost his eye so he had but one left to view my
treachery. Words sprouted blows. Soon we were
battling on the deck.

I struck him on the face and split his lip. He
seized a pin and clouted me so hard I could not
see for blood. The pilgrim women cried for help.
The timbers creaked beneath our scuffling feet. The
end came when he took me in his arms, and if he'd
dashed me to the boards, I'd lie there rotting yet.
Instead he raised me high above his head, then
slowly spun me once around and heaved me head-
long in the sea.

"Until we meet in Hell!" he cried across the rail
and spat.

"Where Mouse stands, Hell is there!" I shouted

back the best I could with three teeth gone. Some-how then I floundered through the swells till, broken both of heart and flesh, I reached the shore at last. It was the first I ever touched the selfsame earth our blessed Savior trod.

The last I saw of Mouse was standing on the deck with one hand raised to shade his eyes. It was as if, for all his wrath, he wanted to make sure I'd landed safe. And thus it came about that with the help of Mouse I saved a city and a king but lost a friend whose like I never found again nor ever hope to find.

Of Wear and Perkin and Godric's tomb.

HERE are the sounds of Wear. It rattles stone on stone. It sucks its teeth. It sings. It hisses like the rain. It roars. It laughs. It claps its hands. Sometimes I think it prays. In winter, through the ice, I've seen it moving swift and black as Tune, without a sound.

Here are the sights of Wear. It falls in braids. It parts at rocks and tumbles round them white as down or flashes over them in silver quilts. It tosses fallen trees like bits of straw yet spins a single leaf as gentle as a maid. Sometimes it coils for rest in darkling pools and sometimes leaps its banks and shatters in the air. In autumn I've seen it breathe a mist so thick and grey you'd never know old Wear was there at all.

Each day, for years and years, I've gone and sat in it. Usually at dusk I clamber down and slowly sink myself to where it laps against my breast. Is it too much to say, in winter, that I die? Something of me dies at least.

First there's the fiery sting of cold that almost stops my breath, the aching torment in my limbs. I think I may go mad, my wits so outraged that they seek to flee my skull like rats a ship that's going down. I puff. I gasp. Then inch by inch a blessed numbness comes. I have no legs, no arms. My very heart grows still. These floating hands are not my hands. The ancient flesh I wear is rags for all I feel of it.

"Praise, praise!" I croak. Praise God for all that's holy, cold, and dark. Praise him for all we lose, for all the river of the years bears off. Praise him for stillness in the wake of pain. Praise him for emptiness. And as you race to spill into the sea, praise him yourself, old Wear. Praise him for dying and the peace of death.

In the little church I built of wood for Mary, I hollowed out a place for him. Perkin brings him by the pail and pours him in. Now that I can hardly walk, I crawl to meet him there. He takes me in his chilly lap to wash me of my sins. Or I kneel down beside him till within his depths I see a star.

Sometimes this star is still. Sometimes she dances. She is Mary's star. Within that little pool of Wear she winks at me. I wink at her. The secret that we share I cannot tell in full. But this much I will tell. What's lost is nothing to what's found, and all the death that ever was, set next to life, would scarcely fill a cup.

It's where I baptised Perkin too. Perkin's not a friend, and hence I did not name him with the five. Ailred. Mouse. The snakes. And Gillian even. What made them friends was this. Fancy us each perched on a different rock in Wear. The water races in between with strength enough to kill. But each of us reached out to touch the other, and our friendship was the comfort of that touch.

With Perkin, it is something else. Instead of standing on a different rock from mine, he is the rock I stand on as perhaps in some way I am also his. I never got a maid with child, or if I did, I never heard. So Perkin is the son I never had.

He's a saucy lad, green-eyed and ruddy-cheeked and fair. He has no special wit with words. His clothes need washing, and his hair's a snarl. He tries to grow a beard, but all that sprouts is thistledown. Often he makes sport of me. He apes my limp and goes *gub gub* to show me how I stammer when I'm overwrought. He doesn't give a whit for holy church, and when I have him kneel for blessing as he goes, he rolls his eyes at me and gapes. Yet how to tell the fathoms that I feel?

Now that I've traveled all these leagues from birth with just an inch or two to creep till death, Perkin is the years I'll never see, and thus my son. But he's the hands that bring me food and drink as well, the arm I need to walk, the lips that teach me cheer, and thus he is my father too.

He helped me make my tomb. He was only a lad of ten or so and I still able then to wield a mallet. I found a great square stone as hard as flint to last. Week after week we pounded it and scraped. We chiseled deep and polished as we went. We never lost a thumb like Ralph the mason, but many a nail turned black from where the mallet missed. The flying powder turned our hair to white. And all the time we'd chat like squirrels or sing so full of mirth that if some stranger happened by, he'd never guess we toiled to hollow out a place where one of us would shortly lie.

Reginald would shake his head and chide.

"For sure, Father," he'd say, "it is not seemly thus. Durham's full of monks who'd deem this task an honor. Or if you choose to make your grave yourself as Jesu hauled his cross up Calvary, there are fitter folk to help you than this popinjay."

Once, as he scolded, Perkin crept behind and wound a vine about his feet so when he made to go, he tripped and sprawled. In courtesy to the robe he wore, I tried to keep a stately face but failed when Perkin climbed a tree and hooted like an owl.

And then the lid. We happened on a slab of rock that Wear had sliced and trimmed it up to size. Then Reginald came to help us put it into place, but just as we were hoisting it, Perkin made us set it down.

"A tomb's like a shirt," he said. "Don't stitch it up until you're sure it's cut to fit. Climb in and see, old man."

Old man is what he calls me to this day, and Reginald always rolls his eyes and groans at it, though as for me, I do not mind. I'm old. I am a man, or was one once. So where's the harm? In any case, I did as I was bade. With one of them beneath each arm, I managed to climb in and lay me down.

"Why look!" cried Perkin. "See, there's room enough for two!" and quick as a wink he clambered in and stretched himself the other way from me. His toe just missed my eye. We didn't tarry long, but while we did, I watched the sky and thought how when my time comes round to lie there till the angel sounds his horn, my tomb will seem less lonely far for knowing that my boy once lay there too.

When I was Perkin's age, I could not write my name, but by that time I'd learned, and thus we carved the letters in that set together in a row spell Godric out. Perkin said there should be something more and with a white stone scratched a likeness of my face, but years of rain have long since washed it out. It was no loss. The face was mostly nose and beard and looked more like a lobster than a man.

He also said we should carve in the year and place where I was born, but I said no. As a man dies many times before he's dead, so does he wend from birth to birth until, by grace, he comes alive at last. Not Wear but far away another river saw the birth of me that mattered most, and the year was the year that Deric died and Godric swam away from Mouse and first set foot upon the holy shore.

Of Jerusalem and what befell Godric there.

DEAR Jesu, teach me how to pray. I know but
little Latin like the priests. Except for Baldwin, I've never spoken to a king apart from thee.
I've never learned to wrap my tongue round courtly
talk. The only words I know are words of earth
and wood and stone fit best for rough, unlettered
folk like me. When people come to gawk at me,
or Reginald comes, or Durham monks, the air is
so a-buzz with words that, when they go, I sometimes do not speak for days. I use my hands instead. One finger set upon my lips means food,
and two mean drink. A wagging back and forth
before my eyes means go. A single hand out-
stretched means come. Dear Lord, were I in such
a wise to pray, I'd have to have a spider's limbs for
hands enough to stretch my need to thee.

What can I tell thee thou dost not already know?
What can I ask of thee thou wilt not give unasked
if that's thy will? Yet I must ask thee even so.
The time I saw Jerusalem, for one. With all that
lies upon thy heart, dost thou remember that?
Didst thou, who saidst God's eye is on the sparrow,
cast thine eye on me? A friar with a cross led me
and other palmers to the sites where thou didst
cruelly suffer here on earth. At each we stopped and

knelt. And every time we did, I felt thy presence near as breath. Oh wert thou near in truth, or was it only that I wished it so?

The friar took us to the court where Pilate had thee flogged and showed us traces of thy blood and fingerprints upon the stone. Then didst thou hear me as I called thy name? Didst mark the tears that trickled down my beard? Oh dost thou hear and mark me now, sweet King? Old Godric has to hope that hope or else his heart, which by thy grace has thumped these hundred years, must crack at last. Amen.

Jerusalem flashed awesome in the sun when I came from Jaffa that first day on foot. She was spread upon the hills, her white walls marked with trees and shrubbery that dived to valleys dark and deep. Her rocky slopes were strewn with olive groves, her domes and towers painted gold and blue. Her roofs were rose and white and green. She was so fair I saw at once how men could die for her as Franks and Turks are dying still, God knows. Still battered from my fight with Mouse, I entered through her gates as in a dream. If so, it was a dream of thee.

How different she was from Rome. Rome was the sights you paid a crook-back guide to show. Rome was the broken bones of ancient times. Rome was goats and owls where once great Caesar's palace stood. Even the holiness of Rome was of another age, for all that passes now for holy there seems dim beside the Rome where Paul and Peter bled. Rome was a city men had built and other men had razed and burned. Jerusalem is God's.

When thou camest riding in upon an ass and

the folk all welcomed thee with shouts of praise and palms, thou saidst if they were still, the very stones would cry aloud instead. And so they do. The streets. The walls. The earth itself. All cries. Rome and her glory were of all things dead. Jerusalem is still alive with thee.

I was the most alone I've ever been. I'd left the *Saint Esprit* and Mouse for good. Deric was no more. Home was a thousand miles away. Of all the pilgrims, knights, and infidels that thronged the streets, there was not even one I knew. Like a snail that hauls his shell upon his back, I carried all I was on mine. And how life loads us down!

Burcwen's bitterness and William's humble kissing of my hand the dawn I left as if he thought he was not worthy even to be called his brother's friend. The lady Hedwic weeping in the night. The cat whose throat I'd slit for martyr's blood in Bishop's Lynn. Poor weaver Small who might be weaving still had I not found him crouched behind that tomb and made him stand to catch the Yorkshire cobblers' murderous eyes. The poor I'd cropped to make them sprout for Baron Falkes, the ones I'd pirated with Mouse. There was no cruel nor witless wrong I ever worked that didn't weigh me down.

And add to that the good I might have done but shirked. Old Cherryman, the priest, who groaned all night remembering his fallen sons. How painless had it been to speak some word of comfort in the dark that might have eased his pain a bit. The wife with child who swung upon her husband's feet. I might have somehow succored her. And all the beggars that I saw in Rome and everywhere, the rack-ribbed children and the blind, the lepers with their loathsome sores. How could I bury treasure deep on Farne that might have bought for each a pennysworth of hope?

Dear Christ, have mercy on my soul. And Aedlward, have mercy too. I've chided you for failing as a father, too spent from grubbing to have any love to spend on me. Maybe it was the other way around, and it was I that failed you as a son. Did I ever bring you broth? Was any word I ever spoke a word to cheer your weariness? All this, and more than this, I bore upon my back from holy place to holy place.

I saw the spot Our Lady met thee carrying thy cross. She swooned and fell. I saw where thou didst wash the dusty feet of those who, when the soldiers came to haul thee off to death, took to their well-washed heels. With a candle in my hand I climbed the hill on which they nailed thee to a tree, thy tender flesh so rent and torn it was more full of wounds than ever was a dovehouse full of holes. In a round-shaped church of stone where knights kept vigil, I saw thy Holy Sepulchre itself, the very shelf they set thy body on. How dark those three days must have been that thou didst lie in death, nor any savior at God's throne to plead man's cause! I kissed a piece of that same stone the angel rolled away to set thee free, and at another church they'd built where thou didst rise to God, I kissed thy footprints in the rock and through an opening in the roof beheld the very channel in the sky that thou didst sail to Paradise.

Then I tramped to the river Jordan where the Baptist baptised thee. A chapel stood on stilts to mark the spot. They were singing mass inside. The voices sounded faraway and soft. Dusk fell. A rope was stretched from bank to bank to help the crip-

ples in who came to bathe in hope the water thou
hadst cleansed as it cleansed thee would make their
bent limbs straight again.

A long-necked bird with spindle legs picked
through the rushes at the river's edge. There was
no one there but him and me and, dimly seen
above, the evening star. I stood and watched the
Jordan flow a while, not rough like Wear but flat
and still. Then waded in.

Oh Lord, the coolness of the river's touch! The
way it mirrored back the clouds as if I bathed in
sky. I waded out to where the water reached my
neck, my beard outspread, my garments floating
free. I let my hands bob up like corks. At sixteen
stone or more, I felt I had, myself, no weight at all.
The soul, set free from flesh at last, must know
such peace.

And oh, the heart, the heart! In Jordan to my
chin, I knew not if I laughed or wept but only that
the untold weight of sin upon my heart was gone.
I ducked my head beneath, and in the dark I
thought I heard that porpoise voice again that
spoke to me the day I nearly drowned in Wash.
"Take, eat me, Godric, to thy soul's delight. Hold
fast to him who gave his life for thee and thine."
When I came up again, I cried like one gone daft
for joy.

"Be fools for Christ," said the Apostle Paul, and
thus I was thy bearded Saxon fool and clown for
sure. Nothing I ever knew before and nothing I
have ever come to know from then till now can
match the holy mirth and madness of that time.
Many's the sin I've clipped to since. Many's the
dark and savage night of doubt. Many's the prayer
I haven't prayed, the friend I've hurt, the kindness

left undone. But this I know. The Godric that waded out of Jordan soaked and dripping wet that day was not the Godric that went wading in.

O Thou that asketh much of him to whom thou givest much, have mercy. Remember me not for the ill I've done but for the good I've dreamed. Help me to be not just the old and foolish one thou seest now but once again a fool for thee. Help me to pray. Help me whatever way thou canst, dear Christ and Lord. Amen.

Of Deric's treasure and Godric's feet.

J ESU walked barefoot up to Calvary, and ever since that day he washed my sins away in Jordan, I've gone unshod to honor him. Unshod, I journeyed home again. Unshod, I tramped the length of England north. Unshod, I found my way once more to Farne, dug Deric's treasure up, and had myself rowed back to shore with two fat sacks I'd strapped across my neck. Their weight was such the boatman charged me half as much again for the return. It was the last time in my life I ever had a coin to pay.

It was the last time too that I saw Farne except in dreams. A mist so thick hung round it that Cuthbert could have stood a yard away and I'd have never seen him. Only the craggy pinnacles rose free, and as we rowed away, a great white bird reared up on top of one and flapped his wings at me as if to say farewell.

A bitter winter rain was falling when we beached, and I took shelter where a tumbled rock gave space enough beneath for me to sit and rest my feet. They were a sight to see! All scabbed and hard and stiff with cold they were, with bloody places where I'd cut them clambering up Farne, the nails grown thick and dark as horn. They looked more claws than feet, and though their grief was mine, I gazed at them as though they were not mine at all. I held them in my hands. I spoke to them.

"Poor feet," I said, "I've used you ill for Jesu's sake. I've tramped with you a thousand miles and more without a scrap of hide to ease your way. I've brought you to this place. I've cut all lines adrift that moored me to the life I knew. I've set myself adrift. So lead me now, old feet. Take me the way that I must go for Jesu's sake. Godric, who's been merciless to you, casts him upon your mercy now."

They did as they were bid. As if some other spirit quickened them, they set themselves upon the road again, and for many days, through rain, through icy moors and woods, they bore me till we reached at last a small, rough church near Bishop Auckland built of stones that some say came from Roman walls. At once I knew it for the place to lay my treasure down for good. I thanked my feet for bringing me. I entered in.

The cold without was nothing to the cold within. The air itself was frozen still as stone. My breath came out in little puffs. No priest was there nor any moving thing except a single candle that swayed upon the altar. I sought to warm my hands at it, but they were grown so numb I could have burned the fingers off and never known. I flung the sacks from off my neck and set them by the candle on the cloth. The priest would come at last and find them there. What he would do with Deric's wealth was God's to know. My only care was that it reach the poor that Deric wrung it from and thus God's will be done at last. Never a man more gladly gave his all away since squat Zaccheus told Our Lord he'd pay back double all he'd ever thieved and leaped down from his sycamore for joy. But even as I made to go, I heard a clatter at my back and turned. Ah Godric, the sights a man has seen he cannot give away like coins, and in the wallet of my heart I finger this one still.

Down from the door I'd entered by there came what seemed at first a beard with legs and arms, a hoary pricklebush that ran. But for the beard, I would have thought a child, such was his height. But for the holy words, I would have thought a fiend.

"In Jesu's name, be off!" he cried. "Be gone!" And as he ran, he clapped his hands before him in the air in such a way as lads chase after butterflies to catch them on the wing.

He darted to and fro. He kicked at things I could not see. He jumped atop a tomb to swat at them. The stoup got in between, and one way first, then roundabout, he played at ring-a-rosy in a rage until he brought his fist down hard and shattered holy water gone to ice.

"I bid thee, *in principio,* fall dead!" he cried. Then crouched and seemed to pick some creature from the floor. "See how I've got him by the tail!"

It was the first he'd taken heed of me, but you'd have thought he'd known me all his life and knew he'd find me there the way he spoke. Between his thumb and finger he held something up for me to see, who couldn't see a thing, though from the moving of his wrist I saw he swung it back and forth.

"This kind's the worst," he said. "They're always small and crabbed like this. See how its tongue lolls out and drips! You mark the stench?"

I marked it well enough but would have thought it was the stench of him who spoke. I doubt he'd washed since the Confessor's day, he looked that old. His wild white beard and hair were snarled with knots and bits of straw and filth. His eyes were ferret sharp. His nose was pinched. He wore a leather thong about his brow. His feet were lashed around with skins. He stood no higher than my chest. He shook his unseen prey at me.

"I spied him creeping through the door," he said. "His master, Satan, sent him here to shit on holy things. Or if a maid should happen by to pray, he'd steal beneath her skirts and work such feats of lechery there to drive her mad. Here's how to deal with such as he."

So saying, he seemed to lay the creature on the floor again, drew up one bony shank and stomped down hard with all his might not once or twice but full three times.

"In nomine Patris!" he cried first, then *"Filii!"* then *"Spiritus Sancti!"* third. "My work is done. The priest can mop the carcass up. And little enough the thanks I'll get." He paused, then said, "Speak, man. What's in these sacks you've left?"

"It's alms long overdue," I said. "It's for the poor."

He said, "Then see the poorest of them all. See a poor body starved and bruised within an inch of death for Christ."

He pulled his rags apart, and there beneath I saw no flesh but only bones with caked and sallow skin drawn tight. He wore an undercoat of rusty chains that must have weighed four stone. I saw where they had scraped him raw.

"For every mouthful I don't eat or drink, Christ gets a mouthful more," he said. "I live on roots and nuts. My drink is rain. Sometimes I roll in nettles or thrash myself with willow wands. For every hour that I sting with pain, Christ stings an hour less. I've got a man's parts same as any man, but save for passing water with, I might as well have none at all. The bliss that I've forsworn on earth but adds to his in Paradise. The children that I never got to keep me now I'm old, the friends I could have made for cheer, they all are his as well. I live alone with wolves and trees. My roof's the leaky sky. I can give to Jesu nothing that I have, for I have nothing left to give, but every worldly good I've ever given up, they're all my gift to him.

"And every demon that I slay is too!" he cried. "There's yet another at the pyx! See him slobber as he bares his bum and squats!" He ran and snatched the empty air again, then swung his arm to dash its brains out on the wall.

Then suddenly he gave a piteous wail and crumpled to the floor.

"He pissed his poison in my ear!" he moaned. "I fear I'm lost."

For the first time then I saw how frail he was. He lay there small and spent. His breath was labored like a feverish child's. I held him in my arms. His smell was foul. All the strength he'd chased his demons with was gone, and he could scarcely raise his eyes.

"Are you another come to torture me?" He spoke so soft that I could barely hear.

"I am your friend," I said. "I'll take you home."

"You'll bide with me a while?" he said. "They're cruelest when I'm weak. They mock at God and Christ. They utter foulness of Our Lady. The lusts and doubts and terrors that they flail me with bite worse than wasps."

"I'll bide a while," I said. "But tell me first your name. Where do you dwell?"

"You're not another fiend?" he said. His eyes were dark with fear.

I said, "No more, I hope, than any man."

He said, "My name is Elric then. I'm an anchorite at Wulsingham. I'll show you where I dwell if you'll but help me there."

I crouched to take him on my back, and when he was aboard, his arms about my neck, he spoke again. "You've left one burden at the altar there and taken on another worse."

"The first weighed more," I said, and it was true. The guilt of Deric's wealth lay heavier far than one old man I bore for charity.

The rain had turned to snow. Before I'd borne him very far, the church was lost to sight in it. He had no breath to spare but with one bony finger pointed me to right or left. Our way led past a hut where a ragged dog leapt forth to bare his teeth and snap at us, but a woman with a shawl about her head came out and when she saw us, crossed herself, and called him off. Some few miles on, we came upon two men out chopping wood. One of them set down his axe and made a ball of snow to hurl at us for sport, but the other, squinting through the flakes, spoke something in his ear, and both took off their caps and bowed for blessing as we passed.

Elric it was, of course, they honored thus, and yet because I wore him like a garment on my back, they honored me as well. It seemed to me the two of us made one. I was the frozen feet, the flesh that bore him like an ass. He was the eyes that spied our way, the soul. What matter if he was half daft and sick and smelled of whiskered age and rot? His very weakness was so much my strength I felt as if without him I'd be only half a man.

The woods grew thicker as we went. What path there was, the snow soon covered it. Wolves howled. The icy branches creaked. The old man's grasp had grown so limp I had to double over at the waist to keep him on. His frozen finger no longer pointed how to go but bobbled useless as a stick. I had to guess the way. It wasn't till we reached a tall and craggy ledge of rock that finally he spoke again.

"Praise God, the cairn!" he breathed into my ear. And there it was—a mound of stones piled shoulder high. On top of it a wooden cross. Behind, the opening of a rock-hewn cave.

I laid him on a heap of skins within and where the earth was blackened made a fire. Without, the wind was wild. Snow danced and glittered at the door. The day was growing dark. The rocky walls were hung with drying herbs and roots and charms to fend the demons off. A cup and bowl were all there was for cheer. Smoke stung my eyes and made them weep. I fetched a cup of snow, and when the fire melted it, I held it to his lips. He drank.

"I'm better now, thanks be to you," he said. "The warmth will give me back my strength. The fiends won't come as long as there is firelight. You needn't stay if you've a mind to go. But if you want a place to rest your bones, you're welcome here."

"Father," I said, "which would you have me do?" An anchorite would choose to be alone, I thought. I had no wish to wreck his peace. And yet he might have need of me, and sure it was that I had need to find some roof against the bitter night.

"I'd have you stay a while," he said, and so I did.

Two years I stayed, and if I never truly loved that small, fierce man whose only love was Christ,

I came to love the life I learned from him. And though I often chafe at it and roar with rage, there's part of me, deep down, that loves it yet.

*Of Elric, demons, and how Godric first
saw Wear.*

ELRIC had studied with the monks. He wrote and
read. He knew the Gospels back and forth. He
had the psalms by heart. An oak grew near his
cave with one great branch he'd climb to like a
squirrel and perch there till he'd sung them through.
He sang in Latin, but, for me, he put them into
speech I understood.

"God keeps me as a shepherd keeps his flock. I
want for nought," he said. "I bleat with hunger,
and he pastures me in meadows green. I'm thirsty,
and he leads me forth to water cool and deep and
still. He hoists me to my feet when I am weak.
Down goodly ways he guides me with his crook,
for he himself is good. Yea, even when I lose my
way in shadows dark as death, I will not fear, for
he is ever close at hand with rod and staff to succor
me."

"Godric," he said, his whiskers stained with berry
juice, "beware the shadows. Never think they're not
afoot because the day is fair. Scratch fair, find foul.
So goes the world. A blue-eyed maid comes in and
kneels by you in church as chaste and pure as
angels are. Your very heart sings praise to God that
such as she adorn this wretched earth. Your eyes
fill up with holy tears to see her at her prayers.

But then, by chance, you touch her with your knee, or else she casts a sidelong glance at you and smiles, and all at once the one-eyed fiend beneath your clothes rears up his lustful head. But for the others praying there, you'd throw her on her back and tup her like a ram though Jesu, carved in wood, looks down on you and bleeds. For what's the blood of Christ to him whose own blood seethes like water in a pot?"

Another time as we were dipping from the spring, he tapped himself upon the brow and said, "My skull's a chapel. So is yours. The thoughts go in and out like godly folk to mass. But what of hands that itch for gold? What of feet that burn to stray down all the soft and leafy paths to Hell, the truant heart that hungers for the love of mortal flesh? A man can't live his life within his skull. His other members harry him. They drag him forth. The Devil and his minions lie in wait without.

"'But worship me, and I'll reward you well,' the Prince of Darkness cries. 'The Prince of Peace, who's he? Your life's to live, not give away to him who's dead and gone these many years and gives you not a groatsworth in return. Christ says, "Take up your cross and follow me." If you would rather follow me, take up a sack to put your treasure in instead.'"

A mouse would nip him or a cramp. Sometimes he'd spew blood. "The fiends again!" he'd cry. "But they have other tricks far worse. Once I was praying at my cairn. Christ came himself, all robed in white. Each finger was a candleflame. His head was ringed with fire.

"'Since all are sinners, I damn the ones I choose to damn and save the rest,' Christ said. 'So are my justice and my mercy both upheld. Thou, Elric, I have chosen to damn. Through all eternity thy fate shall be to suffer pain unspeakable and thus to show my glory forth.'

"I said, 'O Lord, I am a sinner sure. I rate no less. Yet night and day I've served thee all these years as best I could. I've sought to quell my wayward flesh with chains and scarcely food enough to fill a gnat. All earthly loves I have foregone for love of thee. Canst thou not find it of thy grace to damn some other sinner worse than I instead?'

"Christ's laugh was terrible to hear. 'Is that how Elric does my will to love his neighbor as himself?' he said. 'For this thou shalt be doubly damned. Thou mayst as well go gobble up what brutish, greedy joys thou wilt while yet thou canst, for the very moment thou dost breathe thy last, thy torment shall begin.'

"Was this the sinners' friend, I thought, the one who healed the sick in Galilee and prayed his Father to forgive us for we know not what we do? All hope was fled. The one who sits upon the mercy seat had proved himself most merciless of all. I would have hanged myself except I feared to hasten to my fiery doom. And then the priest who shrived me saved my soul.

" 'Poor fool,' he said, 'the Devil often comes in such a guise. Our Lord would never speak so cruel. The next time, take a piece of dung and fling it in his face. Then you will see.'

"So when Christ came again, or so I thought, I winged a turd that caught him on the snout, and sure enough he was not Christ. His white robe fell, and underneath he wore a pizzle like a mule. He had a pointed tail and serpents' scales. He howled at me and fled. Thus does the Devil seek to thwart our faith with lies. Godric, be ever on your guard."

I knew there was some truth in what the old man taught. Devils plague the world like rats indeed. With yellowed teeth they nibble at our souls. They leave their droppings on our holiest ground. They make foul nests in us and gnaw in two the stoutest bonds of love. I thought of the bitter blows I'd had with Mouse. I thought how Burcwen sought to wound me when she didn't come to say farewell the dawn I left the manor of my lord. I remembered my wretchedness the day I prayed for Aedlward in Rome and thought that Jesu had not answered me when all the while it was some devil blocked my ears. These devils turn our love to lust, our humbleness to pride that we are humbled so, our hope in God we cannot see to doubt that God is there to see at all or cares a whit if we be saved or lost. Such fiendish wiles as these old Elric saw and taught me well, but there was also much he did not see.

Shadows he saw everywhere, but never light. Devils were his everlasting prey. With rocks he brained them. He smoked them out with evil-smelling herbs or pelted them with dung. He lashed them from his flesh.

"But what of angels?" I asked him once. "Tell me of them."

He crouched there chewing on a root. He cocked his head at me and spat.

"Each devil keeps a pair of golden wings to gull poor simpletons like you," he said. "Beneath their angel gowns, they're hung like bulls and stink."

Nor did he heed me when I told him how it must have been an angel led me first to Farne. I did not speak of Gillian, of how she bathed my feet and crept beneath my cloak, for fear he'd say she only tempted me to lust. The way the porpoise spoke to me, the way my poor feet guided me to where I rid myself of Deric's wealth—if I had told how angels tended me at times like these, he would have mocked me for a dunce.

Poor Elric, he was old and sick. Even when he ate, he grew more thin. He said there was a demon in his belly that sucked all nourishment. He showed me how a man could feel the creature's hard, round head inside by setting a hand beneath his nether ribs. Sometimes he would roar with pain and retch. But from all he said, I think that even when his health was sound, he'd ever been a grim and bitter man.

"Rejoice!" says the Apostle Paul. "Rejoice ye always in the Lord. Again I say rejoice!" I think that Elric never did. He had no doubt that there were joys awaiting him in Paradise for all his grief on earth, but he'd lived so long in pain and penitence I feared that when his time for bliss came round at last, he'd find he'd lost the art.

Perched in his oak, he'd sing his psalms. "Make joyful music to the Lord with harp and horn and melody! Let the salt sea shout! Let all the waves toss high and clap their wild blue hands! Let shaggy mountains stomp their feet!" But he looked so sour even as he sang, it was as if the sound of all those merry revels hurt his ears.

I did what I could to cheer him. When he grew too weak to walk, I served him hand and foot. I fed him milk to sooth the demon in his belly. I washed away his bloody flux. When he saw devils pissing on his cairn or dancing lewdly when he prayed, I'd make as if to drive them off. I was his Reginald though God well knows I had more thankfulness from him than ever Reginald has had from me.

I told Elric once about a dream I had. I dreamed of Wear though I had yet to see it with my waking eyes. I saw its rocky banks and heard its song. I wandered through green shade. I touched the bark of trees. Cuthbert was there. He took a stick and pointed to a patch of ground whence you could see the river's bend. Ferns stirred and snowy campion. I took at once his meaning. This was where I was to roost at last. Was it not so? I asked without a word. He nodded yes.

With nothing but this silent nod, he made me know that like a guillemot in flight to Farne, I must not tarry anywhere until I found that certain place where I belonged though I should tramp a thousand miles. He broke his stick in half and set the two parts on the earth where they became a pair of snakes. Fairweather was the name of one, the other Tune. I knew them well as I knew mine was Godric. Cuthbert winked one eye at me. He waved farewell.

When I told Elric of my dream, for once he didn't say that I'd been cozened by the fiend. He said, "You'll be a hermit then like me. Those trees will be your house. You'll wear the river for your scarf. The sky will be your cap, the rain your cloak. The snakes will teach you watchfulness. In time, by grace, you even may find happiness as I have found it here."

"I never knew you had," I said.

"Nor yet did I till now I know that I must leave it soon. I'll miss it sore when I am dead and gone.

How many things I'll miss!"

Months later he caught an ague so fierce that even by the fire where I'd laid him wrapped in skins, he shook with cold. Many times he tried to speak to me, but his chattering teeth would not be still. At last he got his message out.

"See them in the shadows there," he said. "They thrash their tails and wring their spiny claws for grief. You'd almost think they were good Christian folk the way they weep."

"Perhaps they weep for you," I said.

He said, "Who knows?" then clutched me by the arm to draw me near. "May God have mercy on my soul," he whispered soft. "I fear in Paradise I'll even miss the fiends."

They were the last words Elric ever spoke. I buried him beside his cairn without his chains. The chains I looped about the oak branch where he'd sung his psalms. To see them hanging empty there cost me the only tears for him I paid. The next day I was up before the sun to seek a place I had no cause, except my dream, to know there was on earth.

How Godric went to Durham, saw two
graves, and nearly died.

Bishop Pudsey summons me to Christmas mass
at Durham. I think he means in part to honor
me, in part to bring some kind of honor on himself
by fishing up old Godric none have seen away from
Wear for twenty years and more. I can scarcely
hobble with a stick. The weather's foul. I'd sooner
have a barber draw my three or four last teeth
than go. But Reginald says I must for Jesu's sake.
Even Perkin chides. He says, "What good is it to
live a hundred years, old man, if no one gets a
chance to gawk at you but rats and owls?" So in
the end I go. My peace goes too.

"First we'll have to swab you down," says Perkin.
"Else they'll think it's not a man we've brought to
mass but the ancient, mildewed carcass of a bear."

Then he and Reginald fetch a pail or two of Wear
and warm them by the fire. I've worn my clothes
so long they cleave to me and fall apart as I am
stripped. They scrub me clean as if to lay me in my
tomb. They free my hair of knots and comb the
cobwebs out. Perkin says they find mouse droppings
in it and a spider's nest. They trim my beard. They
pare my nails. They sprinkle me with rosewater

like a bride and deck me out in garments fresh. I let them set aside my iron vest so I can move more easily, but when they try to place a pair of sandals on my feet, I balk. For fifty years or more I've gone unshod. I won't change now.

They load me on a cart made soft with straw, and Perkin sits astride the mule. Reginald tramps along beside to catch me should the jouncing jounce me off. Snow falls. The sky is grey. The air is damp and chill. On such a day as this, I think, our Savior first saw light while, all about the manger, beasts knelt down to worship him.

When we enter Durham's gate, folk gather in the streets to see me pass. Some ask my blessing, and I raise a hand so milky clean I hardly know it's mine to sign them with the cross. Some snatch at bits of straw as charms against the evil eye. A fat man tries to cut a snippet from my cloak. I catch him in the belly with my heel. Bells ring. Dogs bark. A child makes water in the street. Women lean from windows waving flags.

A blind man in a bonnet, led by friends, begs me to touch his eyes that he may see. I place my thumbs on them. His lids go flitter-flutter, but I mark no greater change in him. He gropes to find his friends again. They catch him when he stumbles on a stone. Some bring me gifts. A pot of honey. A kerchief worked in silk. A basket with a guinea-fowl that struggles free and flaps off cackling through the air. They shove and stomp to touch my clothes. I close my eyes and pray.

Dear Father, see how these thy children hunger here. They starve for want of what they cannot name. Their poor lost souls are famished. Their foolish hands reach out. Oh grant them richer fare than one old sack of bones whose wits begin to turn. Feed them with something more than Godric here, for Godric's no less starved for thee than they. Have mercy, Lord. Amen.

Flanked by monks, the Bishop waits on the cathedral steps, his mitre white with snow. Reginald and Perkin help me up to him, and when I kneel to kiss his ring, it takes all three to hoist me back upon my feet. Hugh Pudsey's barely old enough to sprout a beard, and yet a bishop and a mighty lord as well.

"It's I should kneel to you," he says.

I say, "Pray don't, my lord, or we'll spend Christmas bobbing up and down like turnips at the boil."

The monks have brought a chair with poles to carry me. I haven't been inside since Bishop Flambard's time. The aisles are vaulted now. The nave is done. Thick Norman columns stout enough to hold the welkin up support the high, dim vaulting of the roof. The columns have been carved around with deep-cut lines like garlands, serpents, crooked vines, each different from the rest. Behind the altar there's a shrine to shelter Cuthbert's bones they carted here, with many stoppings over many years along the way, from Lindisfarne.

Even the flames of many candles can't light up this awesome dark, nor all the gathered throng of priests and monks and lords and common folk fill up this emptiness. The hooded monks chant psalms as we wend slowly down, but all their voices raised at once are but the rustle of the wind through trees, the call of owls, in this vast wood of stone. The towns the Conqueror razed when he came harrying the north, the crops he burned, the beasts he felled, the Saxon folk he slew, all haunt these Norman shadows. The silence is the sum of all their voices stilled. As long as these stones stand and this great roof keeps out the rain, Durham's cathedral will be dark with death.

They set my chair down near the altar. Reginald rejoins his fellow monks and takes a choir stall. Perkin stands by me. He whispers in my ear, "If you grow weary, tug my sleeve. I'll cart you to a tavern on my back, and there we'll raise a cup to Christ."

I set my finger to my lips and scowl, but I am glad he's there. His face is all aglow with candelight. His eyes are young and Christmas-bright. The Christmas mass begins.

"Lux fulgebit hodie!" they sing. "The Lord is born to us! *Wonderful* shall be his name, and *God,* the *Prince of Peace,* the *Father of the world to come!"* And even as their monkish voices dip and soar like doves, I see with my heart's eye the steaming dung of beasts, their cloudy breath, the cloddish shepherds at the door. I see the holy mother gazing down, and there among them, in the straw, the freshborn king.

An easy thing it is to love a babe. A babe asks nothing, never chides. A babe is fair to see. A babe is hope for better things to come. All this and more. But babes grow into men at last. That's where it turns a bitter brew. "He hath no form or comeliness," Isaiah says. "No beauty that we should desire him. A man of sorrows we despise." Christ minds us to be good, to feed his sheep, take up our cross and follow him with Hell's hot fires if we fail. All this and more our Savior bids when he becomes a man, and to a man we say him nay. Thus when the Bishop tenders me with his own hands Christ's flesh and blood, I slobber them with tears.

"Bear up, old man," says Perkin in my ear.

But there's more here than can be borne. The gorgeous robes of priests. The altar all aflame. The clouds of incense rich and sharp. And in the midst old Godric, keeping Christmas, blubbers like a child.

When mass is done, I ask to see Saint Cuthbert's shrine.

"Fifty years ago when Ranulf Flambard brought him here," Hugh Pudsey says, "they opened up the chest. It was a miracle. Instead of bones and dust inside, they found a body uncorrupt. The joints were flexible, the flesh so succulent it only wanted breath to live again without a soul. Though he'd been dead five hundred years, his very funeral weeds were still so new it was as if death had not even dared to pluck him by the coat."

The Bishop looks for me to marvel at this wondrous thing, but the miracle of flesh unspoiled by death looks small beside the miracle of that pure soul unspoiled by life who came to me with Glythwin in his arms on Farne.

On the way home, I see another grave that moves me more. This grave is Burcwen's.

There is no stone to mark it, but a nun who'd been her friend shows us the way. It lies within the convent wall. A holly tree grows near. I stand with Reginald and Perkin, one on each side, to prop me up. My fine clean clothes aren't half as warm as rags. My old bones rattle. There are snowflakes in the air.

"She lived and died a maiden chaste," says Reginald. "And now through all eternity she'll sing with other virgins at the throne of grace."

"Poor heart," I say, "if that's the case, she's doomed to die a second death of weariness. She never cared for virgins worth a fig. Besides, she never held a tune."

"How did she come to die?" asks Reginald so he can write it in his book.

"She died of that which slays us all," I say. "They call it life. Be off! Leave me to speak with her a while."

They both withdraw a pace or two and turn their backs. Outside the wall, I hear the harness of the mule. A grey squirrel flicks his tail at me, then flees.

I say, "Well, Burcwen, it's been many years. You'd never know me now. Yet I have not forgotten you nor ever shall. How often I think back upon that night you came. The years have sieved the darkness and the shame so much away that most of what is left is light. Have you and William met in Paradise, and has he pardoned us? Have angels taught him to be still at last? Give him my love if he'll take such a gift from me. And you I send a holy kiss. How old I've grown! I sometimes think that I'm already dead and only dream I live. If God is good, it won't be long. Oh pray for me that often prays for you. Know peace at last, my dear."

"You'll catch your death," says Perkin. Then they take and cart me home to where, as things turn out, my death comes close to catching me. It happens thus.

Unseen by us, four Scottish brigands trail us through the wood. When we reach home and fall asleep, they fall on us and tie us fast with rope. Perkin's mouth and Reginald's they stuff with straw against their crying out.

"We know that you've got treasure here," the leader says. "If you won't show us where it's hid, we'll beat you till you tell."

The weariness and terror of my flesh have struck me dumb. I can't get out a word. I lie there like a heap of rags. They curse at me. They pound me with their fists. They kick me sore. At last I swoon.

When I come to, it's daylight. They have gone. My cup and bowl lie broken on the floor. Before they left, they pissed the fire out. They've slit my heifer's throat for spite. Perkin soothes my wounds with flax. Reginald kneels by me and weeps. My speech comes haltingly.

"Did they but know," I say, "the only treasure old men have lies buried deep in graves."

Perkin says, "You're tough, old man. You'll live another hundred year for sure."

I say, "Though I deserve it, God would never be so cruel."

So Christmas comes and Christmas goes, and the world the holy child is born to rests, as ever, full of dark so deep that all the Norman bishops in the land with all their candles aren't enough to drive it back an inch.

How Godric kept Saint Giles's door and
went to school.

"How old were you when Elric died?" asks Reginald.

"Buck, buck, begawk," I cackle. I flap my arms like wings. "If years were eggs, by then I'd laid some forty-odd."

Reginald shuts his eyes to work his sum. He counts out on his fingers. "So Henry the First was king," he says. How pleased he is to know.

"Cockadoodledoo!" I crow. "The wisest thing that old cock ever did was clap Ralph Flambard in the Tower. I've heard it from his own lips how he got away. He made his jailers drunk, then took a rope his friends had sent him in a cask of wine and swung down from his window like a mitred ape. They say his mother was a one-eyed witch."

"But Henry lived to pardon him and give him Durham back," says Reginald.

I say, "Thus apes are always kind to apes."

Monk Reginald heaves a sigh. "Bishop Flambard, Father, was ever kind to you," he chides. It gives him cramps when folk speak ill of kings and bishops, so I speak more.

"It's as I say," say I. "All apes are brothers. They scratch each other with their tails."

"Didn't Flambard give you leave to make your cell at Finchale here?" he says.

Finchale is the name by which these woods of Wear are known. It rhymes with *wrinkle*, which is just. Had I a coin for every wrinkle that I've minted here, I'd be as rich as I am rucked.

"It's true," I say. "Finchale's part of the rich lands he owned as shepherd of the poor. He and his tonsured monks had godly sport here riding after stag and boar. He'd brain them with his bishop's crook, they say, and strangle with his stole."

"Yet of the goodness of his heart, he gave this place to you," says Reginald.

I say, "Perhaps he sought to make amends for how he dealt with me at Bishop's Lynn."

Reginald knits his brow. He sucks his quill. "Bishop Flambard. . . .? Bishop's Lynn. . . .?" He blushes like a backward lad in school.

"You dunce! You *monk!*" I cry. "Is your life of Godric then so dull and dry you've dozed through it yourself?"

He hangs his head.

I say, "In Bishop's Lynn it was this selfsame Ranulf Flambard, Ralph the Torch, that fired me forth when I was peddling martyr's blood. He burned so hot for William Rufus then, he feared my trade might cost the king some Jewish geese that laid him golden eggs."

"Pardon, Father," Reginald says. "I do remember now."

Then all at once I rue what I have said. "My tongue has been my only blade so long, it's over sharp," I say. "Pay me no mind. Ask on."

He smiles so gratefully I see that by my churlishness, then asking pardon afterward, I've only made him love me more, alas.

"When Elric died, the Lord led you to Flambard

next and thence to Wear?" he said.

I say, "Not right at once. The Lord was in no haste. He let me dally on the way."

Reginald dips his quill. He says, "Good Father, where was that?"

"Good son," I say, "I went to school."

He thinks I jest. The truth is it's the first time since he came that I've been grave.

From Wulsingham, where Elric made his cairn, I wandered north to the parish of Saint Giles, and who should be the priest there but a kinsman of Tom Ball! He even looked like Ball a bit. He had no eye like Ball's that skewed off on a starboard tack, but he was just as fat and slow and damp with sweat. He even knew the manor of my lord. His name was Littlefair. His wife, whose name was Joan, was deaf, and he so used to shouting in her ear he near to deafened all the world as well. His mildest words would set cups jigging on the shelf.

"Friend Godric!" he said. "In memory of my cousin Ball, stay here with us! Saint Giles could use a man like you to ring his bells and keep his door! You'll dwell beneath our roof! Why not? My Joan will feed you for your pains!" He clapped me on the back, his cheeks so flushed with kindliness I had no choice but answer yes.

Littlefair was great of heart. My tasks were many, but he used me well. I'd sit within Saint Giles's porch to mark who entered and who left. I kept a watch for thieves who lusted for Saint Giles's plate. When poor folk came for alms, I'd go fetch Littlefair, who like as not roared counsels in their ear but gave them pence as well. Or I'd get Joan, who read their hunger on their lips and gave them bread.

I saw to it the stoup was filled for christening. Many's the wedding that I swept the floor, and when folk breathed their last, I tolled their knell. For this it was Great Bess I rang. She was as big around as Littlefair himself and six times louder. What a voice! She filled the neighboring air with slow-paced notes so stately, deep, and clear the dead marched with a prouder step to Paradise. Yet at great feasts, with Digory and Little Will to chime her to a fit, she sang for joy.

It also fell to me to tend the lads who sang at mass lest, left alone, they'd tear Saint Giles to bits. They chirped and fought like sparrows in a trap. They'd steal up with their candles from behind and drop hot tallow on bald pates. At Pentecost they brought a cage of mice. They set them free. The women shrieked and held their skirts. One whiskered villain ran off with a morsel of the Host and scuttled up a drain. They puffed their cheeks with air and mocked at Littlefair behind his back or cupped their ears like Joan and hooted out, "How's that again?" I caught them once at unclean acts behind the crypt. And yet it was like angels when they sang!

Their high-pitched voices rose as pure and cool as stone. If sound were something you could see, you'd say they filled Saint Giles with shafts of silver light. And sure it was, it filled your eyes with silver tears to hear them sing the psalms.

Although I thrashed them many times, they seemed to like me well enough. At least they liked the tales I told of sailing on the *Saint Esprit* with Mouse. Their eyes grew wide to hear how we had broken through the Turkish fleet at Jaffa with a royal king aboard. I told them about Falkes de

Granvill too. I made no mention how he cropped the poor or cruelly used his Saxon wife or hanged that wretch for stealing eggs. Instead, I merely spoke of all the wealth and castles that he owned, his stables and his mews, and in the greenwood how he glittered hunting stag. Of Elric too I told them but without his fiends, and how I went to Rome but nothing of the beggars or the stench. How seemly is a life when told to children thus, with all the grief and ugliness snipped out. I suppose it's how monk Reginald will tell of mine.

They knew I was unlettered, and a boy named Gilbert with a freckled face took pity on my shame. "Master Godric," he said, "why don't you come and learn with us? At Saint Mary-le-Bow in Durham, the monks keep school. Perhaps they'll teach you too. Why don't you ask?" I said I would.

Littlefair put in a word for me as well. He told them we were cousins. He said I was a man who'd seen the world and sought my betterment. He said I'd lived with Elric, for they knew his fame, and was given much to fasting and to prayer. He told them too I'd help keep order when the lads went mad. They said they'd ask the bishop then, and thus, though we'd as yet not seen each other with our eyes, my path and Flambard's crossed again. I went to school.

I learned my letters from a cross where they were written underneath a shield of horn. I learned to scratch my name in wax. Each day the monks would ask us, "Who are you before me here?" and we'd chant back, *"Nos pueri."* We are boys. And what a boy I was with grizzled hair and beard to match, my face all rough from years at sea, and yet the dullest of the lot. But Gilbert helped me. I worked hard. Day after day we'd chant the psalms in Latin till I knew them all, together with the great *Te Deum, Nunc Dimittis,* and the Creed.

I learned the *Pater Noster* too, but kneeling by my cot at night, I always prayed it in our own rude tongue. *Father in Heaven, holy one, come be our king that we may do thy will below as they above.* As often as I said it too, I thought of Aedlward and prayed by now he'd climbed his ladder to the topmost rung so both my fathers might dwell side by side in Paradise.

One day in summer Bishop Flambard came, as was his wont from time to time, to see the school. Saint Mary-le-Bow was all agog. The floor was freshly swept and scrubbed, the holy vessels shined. Littlefair and Joan tramped from Saint Giles a mile or so away. Saint Mary's priest went clucking everywhere lest something go awry. The monks lined up the dozen lads they taught, and I stood off a bit apart for fear the sight of one old bull among so many calves might make folk laugh.

Then Flambard entered, taller by a head at least than any there. His hair was flaming red. He reeked of wine. To my astonishment I was the one he came to first. He took my hand in his. He said, "I started low like you and ended high. I doff my cap to any man who seeks the same."

Then I knelt down and kissed the ring of him who back in William Redhead's time was the mightiest man in England save the king, and feared and hated still. When Flambard was Lord Chancellor, they say, all justice slept and money ruled the land. Perhaps it did. I only know that with a hand beneath my chin, he raised me up and smiled.

Of Ranulf Flambard and a dream come true.

FLAMBARD's hands hung at his sides like hams. His belly was a sail puffed great with wind. His feet were cockboats and his stride so long you couldn't walk with him but feel you were a puppy on a string. On top he wore that crop of flaming hair from which some said he got his name. Flambard in Norman means the *flame* or *torch*. Some say, however, that they named him thus because what was on fire was his greed. The more it swallowed up, the more it blazed. Not all the gold and power in the land could keep it fed. And yet to me he ever was most bounteous, as Reginald truly said. I think perhaps he saw in me the seeds of what he was himself and sought to water them.

"You've learned to read and write," he said. "That's well. But don't stop there, my friend. Pile stone on stone. That's how a man must build his life. Keep piling till your battlements o'ertop all else. 'For unto everyone who hath will more be given,' as our Savior said. Christ Jesu never spoke a wiser word. Might begets might and riches riches. That and no other is the truly golden rule."

It pleased him many times to take me with him through the Durham streets and show me what he'd wrought and planned on next.

"These walls are tumbling down, you see," he

said. "For one, they're old as sin. For two, un-counted years of frost have worked their way into the joints and cracked them wide. The town will soon lie open like a woman dozing in a field with legs apart. Already I have masons working night and day to make them safe again. Believe me, scholar Godric, Ranulf Flambard won't be diddled by some villain while he sleeps."

Sometimes we'd go on foot. Sometimes he'd have his servants fetch me forth a horse, and we'd go trotting side by side. But either way his wineskin always came along. Each time we stopped, he'd take a swallow deep enough to drown a cat yet never stumbled or grew thick of tongue.

"To ford the Wear, men wet their feet," he said. He pointed down from where we stood high on the hill where men on scaffolds worked to raise the nave. "To wet the feet is fine for beasts, not men. I'll have them throw a bridge from bank to bank." He waved one huge, red hand as if to throw it there himself. "Then let Wear rage and spew his fill, we'll cross no whit less dry."

Another time he tramped me through the poor, mean huts that clustered near where the cathedral stands. He said, "One wayward spark would be enough to set them all ablaze. And what of God's house then? Of Cuthbert's bones? That piece of Jesu's manger, Moses' rod, and all the other holy gauds folk travel miles to see? Six months from now I'll have this ground all clear, and not one hovel left to tell the tale."

"But the poor who dwell here now, my lord?" I said. "What's to become of them?"

He said, "I'll give them alms to go starve some-where else. It's not the poor that Flambard's famed for using ill. It's other fat, rich rogues like him."

The lofty nave was where we sat the day he spoke to me of times to come, a flagon at his side. The masons with their hammers made a lofty din. They wound stone high on hoists. White dust lay everywhere like snow.

"Godric," he said, "this place will stand a thousand years. Just think what changes it will see! Wonders we can scarcely dream will come to pass. Time was, men had to heave such stones as these by hand. Now they have wheels and rope. What will they have five hundred years from now or ten to make their labor lighter still? We travel now by foot or horse or ox-drawn carts. Someday perhaps we'll make us wings and fly like birds. We'll fix our carts with sails. We'll learn to snare the power of the sun in nets, turn winter into summer, night to day. Godric, we've got kings to rule us now, some well, some ill. The day will come we'll rule ourselves for good. You'll see." He filled another cup.

"Godric," he said, and drained it off, "but breathe one word of this, I'll have you hanged. But this I say into your secret ear. You know where God rules now? Not in churches hewn of stone like this, nor yet in Heaven if the truth be known. He rules within the privy parts and wit of men. With privities we make us others like ourselves as God made Adam once. With wit we'll make a new and wondrous world as God made this one long ago that now grows old and stinks."

He turned his flagon upside down. "Hey nonny!" he said, "the well's gone dry." Then cupped his mouth and shouted to a mason high above, "Don't work too fast. There's lots of time!" Then added just to me, "And lots I mean to fill it with."

He filled it full enough, but there was less time than he thought. In fifteen years his health began to fail. He had them carry his great bulk into the church where he did penance for his grievous sins and left his ring upon the altar as earnest of his vows to mend. When he grew worse, he gave his riches to the poor. He even paid his debts. Then praying to a God he must have hoped by then ruled elsewhere than the carcasses of mortal men, the flame went out at last, and Flambard died.

All this came later though. Those days when I first knew him, he was hale. He loved the chase and often had me come along. I'd ride a chestnut mare and he a broad-beamed roan of seventeen hand to bear his weight. He dubbed him Rufus for the king and wetted down his mash with wine to heat his blood. I cantered in his train of priests and lords and servants chanting Latin verbs or verses that I'd learned in school.

"Don't be so monkish, Godric!" he once cried. "No beast was ever caught with psalms!" and I cried back, "So please my lord, I'd sooner that the beast caught me than face my master with my work undone."

One fair, warm day the Bishop laid a feast for us within the wood. When drink had made him merry, he stripped for wrestling with his friends. His chest was thick with golden hair, his legs and arms like trunks of trees. He snorted like a bull. One by one he threw them all who challenged him, then poured a wine flask on his head to keep him cool. This done, he laid him down against a rock and fell asleep.

The forest floor was dappled by the sun. The air was sweet. The leaves were newly green. When I had wandered off a way, I paused to listen to the sounds of spring. A bird piped from some hidden perch. Back where the Bishop and his huntsmen dozed, I heard the nickering of their steeds. Small, bright-winged creatures buzzed above a pool of rain. And farther off, as soft as sea in shells, a quiet, mirthful murmuring. I thought, could it be voices calling me? Or elf folk dancing in a ring?

I left the path and followed with my ears until the thicket grew so dense I had to crawl on hands and knees. I barked my shins on roots and stones, but still the murmur, ever louder, drew me on. Then all at once I pushed a low-hung branch aside, and there before me lay the place that Cuthbert showed me in my dream.

There was the Wear. There were his rocky banks. There was the little rise where you could see him bend. And there, looped from a branch like Elric's chains, were my two friends. I knew them in a trice. They raised their heads and shot their crimson tongues at me for love, and from that day I knew that here was where I'd live whatever years were left, and here I'd die.

And when I asked his leave to make my cell there, Flambard knew it too.

"Well, Godric, I had grander dreams for you," he said. "I thought you'd heap up riches such that folk would gather in the streets and bare their heads to see you pass. I thought you'd come at last to serve the King."

"And so I shall, my lord," I said. "The King."

He took my meaning then, I think. "If ever he should cast you out, you come see me," he said, whereat he seized me in his arms and hugged me like a bear.

How Godric filled his time, and certain
holy sights he saw.

I'VE lived at Finchale fifty years, and thus my near
a hundred, give or take, are split in two, The first
half teems with places that I saw and deeds I did
and folk I knew. The second half I've dwelled here
by myself. Three times only have I left, such as the
day I went to Christmas Mass at Durham. Except
for those the monks give plaited crosses to, I've
scarcely seen a living soul apart from Reginald, and
Ailred now and then, and Perkin, God be praised.
The lad is twenty-some and started bringing eggs
to me when he himself was little bigger than an
egg. So, by the reckoning of men, one half my life
has been an empty box. Yet if they only understood, it's been the fuller of the two. Three things
I've filled it with: *what used to be, what might have
been,* and, for the third, *what may be yet* and in
some measure *is* already had we only eyes to see.

Voices that I haven't heard since I was young call
out to me. Faces long since faded bloom afresh.
Legs that barely hold me up grow strong again in
dreams to carry me wherever I would go and where
I wouldn't too.

"That hermit Godric!" people say. "How holy
must he be to rest in one place, rooted like a tree, so
he may raise his shaggy arms to God alone while

holy thoughts nest in his leaves like birds."

They do not guess that in my mind I'm never still. Seven times seven are the seas I've sailed in less times than it takes to tell. I can draw my breath on Dover Road and puff it out again in Rome. And oh the thoughts that come to roost in this old skull!

When I'm awake, I'm master of them well enough. Let some woman that I lay with once come chirping lechery in my memory's ear, I've but to clap my hands and she will usually fly away. Or let some ancient grievance croak, some long forgotten hunger whet his beak for more, some foolish pride start preening in the sun, and I've such arms as these old pot-lids that I wear for vest, or icy Wear, or holy prayer, to fend them off. But hermits sleep like other men, alas, and in the dark all men go mad.

Oh what a crop of sons the seed I've spilled in dreams would raise! How many silken coverlets I'd need to cover all the naked flesh I've dallied with in lust though lying all alone the while in rags with calluses thick as cobbles on my knees from prayer. Sometimes maids whom, in the daylight world, I held in such esteem I wouldn't have so much as thought to kiss them save in greeting or farewell, in sleep I've sported with so shamelessly that when I waked, I wept to think on what I'd done. Even to the priest who comes to shrive me now and then, I can't bring myself to name their names. Dear Lord, strew herbs upon my hermit's dreams to make them sweet. Have daylight mercy on my midnight soul.

After such fashion I fill the box of empty years with thinking back on how things were—some good, some bad—and dreaming into life again what's dead and gone. The things that might have been have less in them of sin, perhaps, and yet they're still sadder in their way. An old man's thoughts are long. He falters back to all the cross-roads of the years and wonders how he would have fared if he'd gone right instead of left.

Suppose I'd not strung Burcwen from a branch that day but taken her along? Suppose some other man than Mouse had ferried me to Farne? What if I'd stayed with Falkes de Granvill and grown rich? Where would I be if Gillian hadn't left me in the wood, or if I'd taken me a wife and settled down? Our children's children's children now might be the ones to bring me eggs and comb the cobwebs from my beard. Say Mouse and I had never fought. Say Aedlward had lived to be not just my father but my friend.

Was it God who led me on the way I went, or was his will that I should take some different turn? Life's a list. Good tilts with ill. The de Granvills of the world grow fat. Poor folk eat earth. Even in his church, the Lord is mocked by lustful, greedy monks and priests that steal. Men travel leagues to see the arm of some dead martyr in a silver sleeve that wouldn't lift a hand to save a living child that's fallen in a well. King wars with Pope, and mighty lords attack the King. Bishops like Flambard are but mighty lords themselves with crosses hung about their necks. When Stephen and Matilda strove together for the crown not long ago, the land went lawless. Castles were filled with fiends that burned and tore and flayed men's flesh for gold while God and all his angels seemed to sleep.

All that is out where men can see. Inside, the same old woes go on. Folk lie sick with none to nurse them. Good men die before their time. Their wives and children weep with none to care. The old go daft with loneliness. The young turn sour. Faith's forsaken. Hope takes wing. And charity, the greatest of the three, is scarce as water in a drought.

And what has Godric done for God or fellowmen through all of this? Godric's war is all within. For fifty years the only foe he's battled with has been himself. Above all else, he's prayed.

What's prayer? It's shooting shafts into the dark. What mark they strike, if any, who's to say? It's reaching for a hand you cannot touch. The silence is so fathomless that prayers like plummets vanish in the sea. You beg. You whimper. You load God down with empty praise. You tell him sins that he already knows full well. You seek to change his changeless will. Yet Godric prays the way he breathes, for else his heart would wither in his breast. Prayer is the wind that fills his sail. Else waves would dash him on the rocks, or he would drift with witless tides. And sometimes, by God's grace, a prayer is heard.

Once I knelt outside my cell at dawn. A mist from Wear had hung the leaves with pearls. I'd scattered ashes on my head. For days I'd eaten nothing but a broth of wild angelica that Elric said kept demons off. "Fair Queen of Heaven," I prayed, "God's turned his back on us for sin. The world is dark. Oh thou, his lady mother, take our cause. Beseech him to forget his wrath. Thou knowest from thy days on earth how hard it is to be a man. If thou wilt only kneel before his throne, he must again be merciful for sure. Hail Mary, Mother, pray for us."

I raised my eyes. A lady all in sky-blue mist stood nigh. She wore a golden crown. Her eyes were pearls. Her voice was like clear water in a brook. And then it was she taught her song to me. Its last words were *Our Lady, maiden, springtime's flower, deliver Godric from this hour.* "Deliver every one of us!" I cried. "Deliver all who call on thee!" Her face grew soft with holy mirth. She bowed her head most graciously and smiled. Then she was gone.

Another time I lay awake at night. Tune was sleeping in his jar. The moon was full. "Lord God," I prayed. "How useless is my life. My flesh is ever prey to lust and pride and sloth. I let folk call me Holy Father though I know myself to be of all God's sinful sons most foul. Even as I speak to thee, a thousand wanton dreams are set to fall on me when I am done. Oh send some saint to save my soul. Teach me how to serve thee right."

Then all at once a shaft of moonlight clove my cell, and in it stood the body of a man. By the leather girdle round his waist, I knew him for the Baptist. He cried, "Burn! Burn! Serve man and God as fire does by driving back the night. Let thy very rage against thy sin burst into flame. Dwell here alone and by hot striving to be pure become a torch to light men's way and scorch the wings of fiends. Seek not saints to ease thy spirit's pain that thou mayst better serve. Thy pain's itself thy service. Godric, burn for God!"

Tune raised his head and hissed. A cloud passed by the hazy moon, and all was black.

One summer day I lay upon the grass. I'd sinned, no matter how, and in sin's wake there came a kind of drowsy peace so deep I hadn't even will enough to loathe myself. I had no mind to pray. I scarcely had a mind at all, just eyes to see the green-wood overhead, just flesh to feel the sun.

A light breeze blew from Wear that tossed the trees, and as I lay there watching them, they formed a face of shadows and of leaves. It was a man's green, leafy face. He gazed at me from high above. And as the branches nodded in the air, he opened up his mouth to speak. No sound came from his lips, but by their shape I knew it was my name.

His was the holiest face I ever saw. My very name turned holy on his tongue. If he had bade me rise and follow to the end of time, I would have gone. If he had bade me die for him, I would have died. When I deserved it least, God gave me most. I think it was the Savior's face itself I saw.

Of those who joined Godric at Finchale
and a grievous loss.

I'D lived at Finchale just about a year when I
waked one morning to a noise like knights in
armor falling down a stair. It was a sight I'll not
forget.

An ox-drawn cart came lumbering through the
trees. A cow was tethered at the rear. The cart was
loaded high with pots, an upturned table, bedding,
several chairs. There were some geese and chickens
too. God knows what else. We'd had much rain that
spring, and thus the man that led the ox looked
made of mud. A pair of women wrapped in cloaks
against the chill bounced up and down as creaking
wheels struck rock and rut. One of them, half hid
by bedding, spied me first. She raised her arm and
called my name.

"There's Godric sure as life!" I heard her cry. "I'd
know that great snout anywhere."

The voice was Aedwen's. At her side sat Burcwen
with a grey goose in her lap. The man tramped on
so caked and spattered I could barely see his face,
but it was William right enough.

They'd come. I hadn't known they would, but
so they had. We laughed, as kinsmen do, with
laughter rooted deep in time. We wept with tears

no shallower. We hugged and jigged. And then at last they told their tale.

Littlefair's wife, Joan, had given tidings of me to a friend from York, who on a trip to Nottingham bestowed them on her aunt, and she in turn on Tom Ball's widow, who made such haste to hand them on to Aedwen that she stumbled on a stile and broke her toe. Thus women's gossip makes the world grow small, and thus they knew both that I lived and where. So much for that.

Then one fine day their house burned down. Not then, but later, Burcwen told me how.

"Godric," she said, "I'm sure they set it off for spite. They've always spoken nastiness of Will and me. We've neither of us ever wed. They say we lie together. So we do. But doesn't Mother lie there too, and like as not between? We're not like royalty with beds for each. One does for all. And Godric, by our Savior's wounds I swear he's never touched me in the night unless by chance in tossing or in getting up to piss. It was at night the fire came. I sniffed the smoke before the flames broke out. Thank God for that. It gave us time to save our goods. We stood there in the dark and watched it burn. Mother swears a part of her burned with it. Godric, ever since, she rattles when she breathes. Her eyes grow dim. Those rogues that thieved her of her house made up for it by adding ten years to her age. May fiery rats gnaw on their bones in Hell!"

Her ears were red with anger. Her eyes were bright. Her face and shape had softened since I'd seen her last, more like a woman now and less a lad in skirts. Her lips were more a woman's too. I thought of how she'd pressed them once to mine to breathe life back in me so long before.

I helped William build a hut for them. It looked more fit for beasts than men but kept the weather out. It gave on Wear, and Aedwen sat for hours in the door to watch it flow.

She said, "There's two things charm the eyes like wizardry. One's flames, but flames I've seen enough to last my life. The other's water. I watch that river till I think I even hear him sing."

When I asked her what he sang, she said, "He sings that all things pass. He sings that winter passes. Then comes spring. The old king dies, they crown a new. Pink-cheeked lads and lasses shrivel up like apples on a shelf. There's not a man alive today but time, like Wear, will carry him off too."

I said, "It sounds a sad song then."

"What? Are you daft!" she said. "Can't you hear him chuckle while he sings? And well he may. Who wants a life that never ends? Not me, that's sure. Who wants a sun that never shuts his eye? Death's like the night we need to rest our bones."

"That we may wake refreshed in Paradise," I said.

She said, "Or never wake at all. Who knows? I only know that life's like porridge. It's good to eat when eating's what you want, but the time comes when you've had your fill."

I said, "The dead shall live again. That's holy faith."

She was nothing like as old as I am now, but sitting in the doorway there, she seemed to me the oldest thing alive. Her eyes were hooded like a hawk's. She had more wrinkles than an old clay wall has cracks.

"Godric," she said, "I'll tell you this. I've labored

all my life. I've baked and brewed. I've woven, spun, and dyed. I've kept my husband's house and raised his young. And many other things besides. So where was time for holiness? What strength was left for faith? Let monks and nuns and priests have care of that. The dead shall rise? The Lord himself will sit as justicer in manor court? It may be true for all I know. But in the meanwhile bread, beer, work, and rest at night, they're truth enough for me."

"But the river of the years will wash all these away at last as you've just said. So where's truth then?" I asked.

"Perhaps truth passes too," she said. "Perhaps that's why the river laughs until he wets the rocks with tears." She laughed herself then, or she wept. Whichever one, she hid it with her hands.

So months went by. William worked the ox to till a bit of ground. He kept the cow. He helped me hew the wood for Mary's chapel. And like his hands, his tongue, of course, was never still. As birds must flap their wings to stay aloft, he flapped it on and on as if, were ever he to stop, he'd perish in the fall.

I speak a word. My friend speaks back. Then I again, then he, and thus we make a bridge of words so each may fetch across the ditch that lies between what's in his heart. But William never paused enough to let the other have his say, for fear, I guess, his friend might flee away instead. Thus no bridge ever crossed from him to anyone. Of all the men I ever knew, I think my brother was the loneliest.

"He works until he drops," said Burcwen. "All the years you were away, he cared for us." I caught the chiding in her words. "Husband, father, brother, he was all three of them at once. He'd give his life if we had need of it. He'd do the same for you."

I said, "You love him, Burcwen. Thank God you do. He has no other."

Her face grew pale. She turned her face away and with one finger in the dust drew rings. At last she spoke.

"Godric," she said, "he drives me daft. He's dull as he is good and true. He's never had a sinful thought. I don't believe he thinks at all. He may well be some kind of cloddish saint, but, God forgive me, every time I see him come, the heart within me turns to stone." Tears filled her eyes. She said, "I've wasted my whole life on him."

For pity then I took her in my arms. "No life's wasted when it's spent for charity," I said.

She said, "My youth is spent. I'll look like Aedwen soon. There's no man cares a fig for me."

I said, "You're fairer than you ever were. There's many men would take you in a trice."

"But not the one I want," she said.

"Who's he?" No sooner had I asked it than I saw at once she did not wish to tell her love. She bit her lip and blushed.

"The Man in the Moon," she said, then gathered up her skirts and ran away.

Winter came. Old Wear froze hard. Snow fell on snow. The woods were still. William trapped small game, but food was scarce. The three of them dwelled in their house, I in my cell. We dug a path between, but it would often lie for days untrod. God was the cause, for he and I were like a couple newly wed. I ever spoke my love to him. I bared my heart for him to cleanse. I sought to please him

149

any way I could, and since there were no riches I could give to him whose coffers hold the sun and moon, I'd give instead by taking from myself.

Elric taught me this. The fire that I didn't build for heat, the wool for warmth I went without, the food I didn't eat—all these were like the trinkets that a man gives to a maid. More precious still, I gave him all the cheer I might have had with other mortals like myself. Sitting by a flaming hearth with bowls of broth and talk of times gone by, how we'd have laughed the winter wind to shame! And yet, instead, I gave it like a bright and fiery gem for God to pin upon his gown or deck some starless corner of the sky.

Knowing what I was about, my kinfolk rarely came to trouble me. They'd always thought me queer as a two-headed calf, and this was but one further proof. The only times we met were those I chose. Except for one black, bitter night.

William woke me.

"Mother's calling out for you," he said. "She says the river's beating at the door to take her off. Come quick!" For once, he had no other word to say, and in his silence I could hear his dread.

They had her swaddled like a child in Burcwen's lap. At first she didn't know me for her son.

"You're Wear!" she cried. "I know you by your icy hand. Your eyes stream down. You smell of death and damp. Be gone!"

But Burcwen soothed her. She said, "It's only Godric, Mother. He's come to say goodnight."

I said, "My dear, don't be afraid. Wear's frozen stiff outside. You're safe."

"Do you remember when we went to Rome?" she said. Her voice came quiet now. She took me by the hand. "Mile after mile we tramped. Green hills. Blue sky. Sometimes you hauled me on your back. Remember Cherryman the priest and Peg? How was that mason called?"

I said his name was Ralph.

"And dainty Maud," she said. "She had an ivory spoon, I think. You plucked me figs."

I said, "How many years ago that was."

"As many as a dog has fleas," she said, then seemed to doze a while as Burcwen smoothed her sparse, white hair. Snow beat upon the roof.

"Come, let's away," my mother said at last, her eyes still shut. "Hitch on your pack. Who knows what dangers lie ahead, but in such goodly company as this we've nought to fear."

"We've nought indeed," I said.

She raised her hand and touched my beard. "And if I twist my foot again," she said, "you'll carry me for sure?"

I said, "As sure as sun will rise and though you journey farther than the moon."

"Then all is well," she said, and in her daughter's arms she died with both her bearded sons at either hand.

Of what befell one summer's day.

MY mother lay in hallowed ground at Durham. I had my snakes and God. Burcwen and William had each other. Wear sang his song. And thus we dwelled for many months. A stranger would have said we dwelled in peace, and in some measure that was so. But sometimes when the sea is calm, a splash, a spewing up of foam, makes clear that monsters churn below.

One summer's day I sat upon a mossy bank. Fairweather lay along a branch. Tune was coiled about my leg and slept. For fear of waking him, I kept as still as death and turned my thoughts to prayer. I praised the Lord for warmth and greenery. I praised him for the shaggy earth, untouched by Adam's fall, that feeds us with his crops though we as Adam's sons deserve to starve and gives us such a soft, sweet couch to rest our heads. I thanked him for the faithfulness of ox and cow and hen who serve our needs though we are often cruel to them.

Then as I sat praying there, I saw my sister come though she did not see me. She walked along the riverbank and when she reached a spot not far away sat down upon a rock. She let the water play about her feet. She picked a pebble up and cast it in.

Why was it that I didn't call to her? It would have wakened Tune, but what of that? I'd often wakened him before, nor did he ever love me less. It's true it would have stopped my prayers, but the sight of her had driven God already from my heart. I don't know why I didn't call. Perhaps it was because we shared a silent peace which I was loath to break with words as louts break glass with stones. Perhaps I feared the turn our words might take out there alone with no one else to hear. In any case, I held my tongue.

After a while she rose and walked a little farther on. Now and then she'd stop to gather flowers as she went. The sun grew warm. She doffed her cloak. A thrush sang somewhere in the leaves. She paused to hear, then knelt down at the water's edge and splashed some coolness in her face. Then rose again and, laying all her clothes aside, went wading into Wear.

Within my mind she stands there yet. Her naked limbs are shapely. Her virgin breasts are pale and soft as doves. Her hair is bright with sun. She stoops to cup some water in her hand. Susanna never bathed more chaste and fair than she, all unaware that not far off the hidden elders looked on her with lust.

Lust is the ape that gibbers in our loins. Tame him as we will by day, he rages all the wilder in our dreams by night. Just when we think we're safe from him, he raises up his ugly head and smirks, and there's no river in the world flows cold and strong enough to strike him down. Almighty God, why dost thou deck men out with such a loathsome toy? Burcwen is a fair, white bird in Wear while, hidden on the bank, her brother burns.

From that day forth I kept away from her. She could not know it was myself I fled. She thought she must have been the one to do some wrong for which I chastened her. As I shunned her, she took to shunning me. She cast her eyes upon the ground. She seldom spoke. She took to eating less and less till one day William came to me.

He said, "I fear our sister ails. Some lettuce or a parsnip's all she takes for days on end. Water is her only drink. Perhaps she grieves for Mother. I don't know. Women's ways are ever strange. A radish now and then. She won't have meat or bread. I hear her moaning in the night. I offered her some hare I'd caught. She turned away. She cooks for me but takes none for herself. Her legs and arms become like sticks. Can it be some witch has cast a spell on her? They say that sometimes maids that have no man to lie with pine away like this. Or else. . . ." and on and on. If I had told him what I knew to be the cause, he'd not have heard. He wasn't listening to himself, I think, still less to me.

I prayed, "Dear God, help me to be some help to her. Anoint my eyes that I may see my sister as a soul in need. Oh open thou the door I've closed between us two that I may tender her the love of Christ."

One day at dusk I came upon her at the spring. She was as William said. Her eyes were fever-bright and she herself so lean she could have been a sailor shipwrecked on a raft for weeks. My bowels within me stirred for pity and remorse, and when she started off to go, as if the sight of her would make me wroth, I stayed her with my hand.

"My dear," I said, "I've used you ill. The sin is mine. Forgive me if you can. Stay here and let me speak my heart."

"Your heart?" she said.

154

Just then I chanced to notice William on his way to fill his jar so I could only whisper in her ear, "Come later when he's off to bed." She nodded gravely that she would.

Reginald, when you sit down to write my life, write this. The worst that Godric ever did, he did for love. Nor was it of an earthy sort that seeks its own but love that gives itself away for the beloved's sake, and thus, when all is said and done, the love that God himself commands.

There was no moon that night, and when she came, it was so dark I thought at first the sound I heard was but the wind until she spoke.

"Since the Man in the Moon would never come to me," she said, "I've come to him."

And then I knew.

How long we lay there, I can't tell. We had the loneliness of years to fill and years of unsaid words at last to say. She told me how the dawn I left in Falkes de Granvill's train, she had not come to bid farewell in hopes I'd go to seek her and be left behind. I told her how her staying off had wounded me.

She said she nearly swooned the day I asked if she would come to Rome but feared that Aedwen on our way might sniff her secret out. I said how many times I'd dreamed about her swinging from that tree as I tramped on, not daring to look back lest I should cut her loose again so she might leave my lord's with me. I spoke of all the windy nights I lay on deck and thought of her. She spoke of how she'd lie awake and weep for fear I'd drown.

I think there was no time like these we did not live again, and in the end I even told how, to my shame, I'd watched her bathe in Wear. She said,

"Dear heart, the shame is mine, for from the start I knew that you were there."

And thus we talked the time away, nor was it only words that passed between us till at last for weariness we fell asleep in one another's arms.

As on the night that Aedwen died, what wakened me was William's voice. He stood outside my cell.

"Burcwen's gone!" he cried. "Did you hear her pass this way? I fear the fever's made her daft. Who knows what mischief she may do herself?"

I could not see the hand before my face, but William's dread I saw. I said, "I've been asleep an hour or more. Since then I've heard no sound." That much at least was true. "I'm sure there is no cause for fear. She probably couldn't sleep, that's all. She rose to count the stars. As like as not she's waiting now to see the sun rise over Wear."

"Those rocks are treacherous at night," my brother said. "I'll go and look for her."

I said, "She'll soon come home, you'll see. You'd best go back to bed." But he had gone by then, and off there somewhere in the night he kept on calling out her name as sometimes to this day I wake and think I hear him calling still.

"Burcwen! Burcwen!" he cried out, now near, now far—the kind of lonely, longing plaint that dogs make, baying at the moon.

She took my hand and set it on her lips as if she feared that she might answer otherwise, and then, so soft that she could hardly hear, I said, "May God have mercy on our souls."

For three days William wasn't seen, as if the dark had swallowed him. And so it had.

A pair of Flambard's monks came out to fish a mile or so downstream and found him floating on his face where Wear had dug a little pool. His arms were flung out wide. Trout nibbled at his clothes. The monks said there was bleeding at his brow. He must have stumbled on the rocks that night and cracked his pate as he fell in. Wear did the rest. And thus Will Wagtongue's tongue at last was still.

So, Reginald, when you come to write out Godric's sins, be sure, although he struck no blow himself, to set down murder with the rest.

Of what became of Burcwen,
Godric's second sight,
and the departure of two old friends.

Aᴛᴇʀ William's death, life never was the same
again. Till then I thought that by God's grace
and praying night and day I'd curbed my grosser
sins at last. Then all at once they broke their bonds.
I lay with her whom ties of tenderness and love and
holy law, all three, forbade. When William asked
if she was there, I foully lied. I lied again by telling
him she'd probably gone to Wear to watch the sun
come up. I let her place my hand upon her lips
which else she might have opened to cry out the
truth to him. And thus I sent my brother to his
grave as sure as if I'd felled him with an axe.

If up till then I'd drawn apart from other folk
to be alone with God, from that day forth I shut
the door and bolted it. In part I thought to save
myself from the calling of the world to sin. In even
greater part, I think, I sought to save the world
from me. For months I talked to none except Our
Lord in tears and penitence. Even Tune and Fairweather, when they came slithering up for love, I
turned away without a word. Like Elric, I took to
flogging my back raw with sticks. When nights

were coldest, I'd go down and sit in Wear in hopes that having drowned poor William, Wear might drown the fiend in me. I fasted. I had them fettle me my iron vest.

And Burcwen. For better than a year she lived on in the house that William made. She grew so thin her cheeks went hollow. The flesh around her mouth and eyes shrank back till you could see the skull beneath the skin. We rarely met, and when we did, we could not speak for shame. I left a cheese once at her door to put some flesh back on her bones, but when I happened by again, the droppings and the greasy crumbs made plain that those who'd nibbled them had had long tails and yellow teeth.

Another time when I was on my knees at night between my cell and Wear, I thought I saw a slender shadow stir. If it was Burcwen, though, she never came. In winter when the snow and ice were fierce, we shook beneath our different roofs alone, and that's what Hell is like, I think. It's cold and shame and shaking. And worst of all, it's loneliness.

For weeks I saw no trace of her. At last I went and looked inside her door. The room was empty. On a shelf lay William's cap and the shirt he'd drowned in washed and folded neat. She'd strewn them with some flowers, withered now. "A kind of cloddish saint" she called him once. This was a shrine she'd made for him with relics watered by her tears. I found no sign that she'd been there for days, and when I gazed upon the bed where she and Aedwen and my brother used to lie, I thought how now for all I knew she'd left this world to sleep with them in death. I walked along by Wear in fear I'd find her as the monks found William

159

or lying like a wounded doe who'd starved for want of food. Then one day as I was hewing wood, she came.

A stout woman with a kerchief on her head stood close beside. Burcwen looked like clothes hung on a stick to keep off crows.

"I've been staying with the Durham nuns," she said. "Sister Hailtun's kindly come to help me fetch my things. The prioress has given leave to take me in as one of them. So I'll be leaving now for good. I'm here to say farewell."

Sister Hailtun had the voice to crack a nut. She said, "The brother lives a holy hermit's life! The sister gives herself to be Christ's bride! How proud the mother would have been of such a pair!" She set her hands upon her hips and clucked at us.

I knew why Burcwen brought her. If we'd been just the two of us alone, we would have either had to say things better left unsaid or ever after rued not saying them. This way we couldn't load our words with more than Sister Hailtun's ears would hold.

I said, "Go in peace then, Burcwen. May God have mercy on our souls and grant us years enough so one day we may meet again."

"Or else may Heaven be our meeting place," she said. "If we can only pray and fast our sins away, perhaps they'll let us slip through good Saint Peter's gate at last."

"With souls as pure as yours already are," said Sister Hailtun, "they'd welcome you this day, or I'll be switched."

"Pray for me, Burcwen," I said.

She said, "And you for me."

I said, "I'll not forget."

"Nor yet shall I, though I should live to Aedwen's age," she said. "Godric, farewell."

"Farewell," I said. We clasped hands for a moment. Then she turned to go. Sister Hailtun's were the only tears. "A parting's like an onion. It brings the water to my eyes," she said. Then she and Burcwen walked off through the trees.

I saw my sister only one more time. By then some fifteen years had gone. Flambard summoned me to Easter mass at Durham. In gorgeous robes he and his fellow priests were breaking up the body of Our Lord in five and sixty pieces. These they laid out on the altar one by one to make a cross of bread while back and forth the monks were chanting psalms. The nave was filled. And as I gazed out over all those heads, I saw Burcwen.

She was standing by a great stone column, her hair itself as grey as stone and other grey nuns all about. At first she didn't see me there, then raised her eyes, and when they met with mine, it was as if all else between was swept away. She was so far we had no way to speak, nor was there any sign to make, but monks would need at least a year with pen and quill to set down all we somehow said. She closed her eyes then, I closed mine, and while the Bishop with a palsied hand poured out Christ's blood, we bade our last farewell.

Soon afterwards I saw the death of Roger Mouse. I had my eyes fixed on the lowering sky when all at once, as if the clouds were waves, I saw the *Saint Esprit*. The wind had rent her sail. Her bow was split. She foundered on the rocks off Wales. Mouse stood on deck alone.

He had one arm about the mast. The water scudded in about his knees. His hair was white as spume. When he opened up his mouth to cry, I saw his teeth were mostly gone. And yet his voice was no less strong than when I'd heard it cursing me at Jaffa years before, nor was it any cry of fear. Instead he gave one wild last shout as if to say Die! Die! as full of zest as once he'd said Live! Live! And then it was he spoke my name.

"Deric!" he cried. You might have thought he saw me kneeling there although with just his one eye left and all that lashing spray I doubt he saw a thing. "Deric!" he cried a second time, and then, before my eyes, the *Saint Esprit* went down for good, and Roger Mouse sank fathoms deep in sky.

I've seen many a shipwreck in the clouds since then—strangers on strange ships undone by storms or dashed on rocky shores. Sometimes in the midst of talking to some folk sent by the Durham monks, I'll suddenly break off and start to weep. They think I'm weeping for their sins or mine or gone stark mad, but that's not it. It's watching men and women lost in gales. It's hearing little children cry in fear as waves wash over them or suck them down to make some monster's feast.

This second sight of mine has ever much to do with death, for either I see wrecks at sea like this, or else I'll look upon a man and see how he's to end his days. While Flambard still was stout and hale, for one, I saw him carried down the aisle and laid beside the altar. There, like a fish unswallowing a hook, he tried to choke out all his sins but choked his life away instead.

And then there's he I cannot name for grief. He wasn't any higher than my knee when I beheld him dead upon a hillside strewn with other fallen men and steeds. He had an arrow in his chest. He held a dagger in his hand. His other arm was crooked across his face, and thus, praise God, I never had to look upon the lad's green eyes that else had shone so bright with life, now blind in death.

I never tell them what I see. It's hard enough to live not knowing when you'll die. The knowing's worse. But those whose ends I've seen ahead, I pray for every day. I pray them strength to meet whatever waits for them. I pray them grace to live such lives as, when death comes, they'll have no cause to fear. And those whose dying comes more cruel than most or comes too soon, I pray the Lord will find instead some easier hatch to hoist them through or have it be that what I've seen is just an old fool's dream.

I was at prayers like these when Tune and Fairweather came. Fairweather coiled about my arm. Tune raised his head and called me with his merry eye to sport with him. When I told them to be off, they paid no heed. Fairweather climbed and twined himself about my neck. Tune beckoned with his tongue and swayed from side to side. At last I had my fill. Fairweather I untwined and set upon the ground. I took Tune by the neck and laid him roughly at his side.

I said, "I've told you both a thousand times and more to let me be while I'm at prayer. I've threatened you. I've warned and pled. And yet you're ever at your wiles. You weave and sway and slide and hiss. You wrap my limbs around like vines about a tree. It's not just me you vex here on my knees. You vex God too. So now enough. I wish you well. But never let me look on you from this day forth. Begone!"

163

They lay as still as sticks, and I had raised my hand to strike when suddenly I saw their eyes were closed and they had bowed their heads. It was their way to ask my blessing as they left. No sooner did I understand, than down my cheeks streamed tears.

"May God go with you, if he goes with snakes," I said. "May summer sun shine warm upon your scales. May winter's rest be deep."

And then they slowly went, my two fast friends, nor have they come back to this day. Oh Queen of Heaven, might I only tame the beasts within myself so well!

How Reginald sought Godric's blessing on
his book, and Godric's death.

I'VE told my life from both its ends at once. Beginning with my youth, I've moved ahead from
year to year. And also, all but ready for the tomb I
hollowed out of stone with Perkin's help, I've wandered back the other way. And now at last both
Godrics meet—the one who was, together with the
one who is, like raindrops trickling down a leaf
to make a third. The third's the Godric yet to be,
the Godric God will raise again to life and either
burn in Hell as he deserves or caulk and patch until
he's fit to sail to Heaven at last.

Reginald's forever after me to hear him read his
book. He says he's written all my years till now.
He doesn't say I've only got a page or two still left
to live, but there's no doubt that's what he means.
He wants my blessing on his work while I've still
breath in me to bless. I tell him that it's bad enough
to live a hundred years and more without the need
to tramp a parchment path back through a second
time.

"Ah well," he says, "there's no cause you should
hear the whole. Father, if you'll give me leave, I'll
read you just a passage here and there. A sip or
two's enough to prove the milk's not sour."

I say, "That it's too sweet is what I fear, but if
you must, read on."

165

Then, as he goes to fetch his scroll, I think how Ailred brought him to me years ago. "Here's Brother Reginald," he said. "Remember how our Savior bids us let our light so shine that men may see the good we do and glorify God's name. I hope you'll tell him everything you can so what he writes may light the way of all who read for years to come." As Reginald kissed my hand, his face was like a sheep's, and when he opened up his mouth, he gave a bleat as now he does again, returning to my cell. He spreads his parchment on his knees.

He reads, *"In winter, barefoot, this holy man would often walk through miles of snow and ice to find some poor, frozen animal which he would bring back and warm in his bosom. Winter and summer both, he would seek out the sick ones and administer medicine to make them well. Observing stags as they were being pursued by hunters, he would invite them into his cell where he would conceal them until all danger was past. Animals of numerous kinds would come running to him for protection, sensing that he was a man of extraordinary sanctity."*

"I took them in to ease my loneliness. It was at least as much for me as them," I say. "And if they ever fled to me to keep them safe, it was because they had no other place to go."

"Such humble speech becomes your holy state," says Reginald. "Now, Father, if I may, I'll read you something more." He licks his thumb each time he turns a page.

"When the boy had passed his childish years in quiet domesticity at home," he reads, *"then, as he began to reach maturity, he resolved to pursue a more ambitious course and to educate himself me-*

ticulously and persistently in the ways of worldly circumspection."

"Write *worldly greed* if you would better hit the mark," I say, but Reginald reads on.

"There came a time," he reads, *"when he elected not the vocation of a husbandman but rather that of a merchant. At first he was content to peregrinate with small wares through the villages of his own neighborhood, but in process of time he did so profit by his increase in age and sagacity as to travel through towns and cities and to fairs in pursuit of public chaffer."*

"He chaffered the blood of one lone cat for many coins, that's true," I say, but by the way he frowns and sniffs, you'd think I'd only broken wind.

"Yet in all things he conducted himself with admirable simplicity," Reginald says, *"and insofar as he yet knew how, he persisted in the footsteps of truth. For, having learned the Lord's Prayer and the Creed from his infancy, he frequently meditated upon them as he went solitarily on his more extended journeys and clung thereunto most devoutly in all his cogitations concerning God. In time he formed a familiar friendship with a certain other man who was eager for merchandise and in his company began to initiate more adventuresome courses and to travel by sea to foreign lands."*

"The only thing that Mouse was eagerer for than wares," I say, "was maids who'd do it free."

Says Reginald, "Please, Father, for the sake of him who is himself the Truth, I leave some small truths out."

"This life you've written down will be the death of me," I say.

"Now, if I may," says Reginald and tips his

parchment to the light. He reads, *"He was subject to many perils on the sea, yet by God's infinite mercy he was never wrecked, for he who had sustained Saint Peter as he walked upon the waves, by that same puissant right arm preserved this his chosen vessel from all misfortune amid these vicissitudes. On his circumnavigations Godric frequently touched on the isle of Farne which Saint Cuthbert had inhabited as an anchorite and where (as he himself would relate afterwards) he would meditate on the saint's life with abundant tears. There he began to yearn for solitude and to hold his merchandise in less esteem than previously."*

The bleat of Reginald becomes the cry of gulls. I see the holy isle again as clear as if I stood upon its rocks. I smell the chill and salt-sweet air. The pinnacles rise out of mist. On top of one, a guillemot spreads wide his wings and beats the sky. I must have sunk into a dream, for Reginald has to pluck me by the sleeve to make me hear.

"Godric was vigorous and strenuous in mind," he reads, *"whole of limb and strong of body. He was of medium stature, broad-shouldered and deep-chested with a long face, grey eyes most clear and penetrating, bushy brows, a broad forehead, long and open nostrils, and a nose of comely curve."*

"They took it for a ship's prow once," I say, "and set to scraping off the barnacles."

Reginald holds up his hand. *"His beard was thick,"* he reads, *"and longer than the ordinary, his mouth well-shaped with lips of moderate thickness. In youth his hair was black, in age as white as snow. His neck was short and thick, knotted with veins and sinews. His legs were somewhat slender, his instep high, his knees hardened and horny from frequent kneeling. His whole skin was rough beyond the ordinary until all this roughness was softened by old age. Such was the external appearance of this saint.*"

"This SAINT!" I cry.

Then there's a roaring in my ears as if all the blood I have in me is sucked into my head at once with pain so cruel I think my skull will fly apart. Reginald goes pale as death and hastes to me. I push him off.

"Blasphemer! Fool!" I cry.

Half blind, I try to crawl away, and when he seeks to succor me, I turn and would have bit his hand had he not leaped aside. And then I swoon.

How long I lay there I don't know, but Perkin's voice I hear at last. "You've gone and fouled yourself, old man," he says. "I'd better fetch a pail and cloths."

His face is near enough to touch. Above him, like a great blue hat he wears, there looms the sky. I try to raise my hand but fail. My tongue will move, but no words come. I see a tear start from his eye, and as it makes its way along his cheek, I know as surely as I know my name that on this day my death will come.

Instead of pail and cloths, I crave to wash once more in Wear. With wordless croaks and groans and rolling eyes I somehow make this clear to him. He hoists me to my feet, and when I find I still can move one leg, he slings my arm around his neck. Then holding me about the waist, he hauls me forward step by step. My jaw hangs partly down. Perkin staggers now and then beneath my weight. My useless leg I drag behind us like a tail. We move like some ungainly beast until at last we reach the water's edge where all at once we start to laugh.

Perkin tosses back his head. I shake so hard I nearly fall. Then, when he slowly lowers me to where I'm in up to my neck, Wear joins our laughter too.

How rough and yet how soft the river's touch! He falls about my shoulders like a silver shawl. He chills me to the marrow of my bones. He leaps and dances in the sun. He washes all my foulness off. And all the while, he slaps his rocky thighs and roars with mirth.

When Perkin hauls me to the bank again, the water runs from me in pools. I can't stand by myself so Perkin holds me underneath my arms.

"I'll take you to your cell and dry you off," he says. "I'll lay you on fresh straw. Then you can rest, and in a few days' time, old man, you'll rise again to dance a jig."

He's just about to pick me up when Reginald appears. He's got his parchment tucked into his sleeve, but seeing me, he takes it out and comes and kneels.

"Father," he says, "God's blessed your life. Will you not bless this little part I've written down for men to read when you are gone?"

I try to speak, but nothing comes save brutish grunts. I feel the spittle on my chin. If I could move my hand, I'd reach and lay it on his monkish pate. If I had legs I still could bend, I'd kneel to beg that he forgive me all the years I've used him ill. Instead I can do none of these. So Perkin, from behind, picks up my hand and hoists it high to sign his parchment with the cross. Reginald bites his lower lip. A mouse goes scuttling through the straw.

This is the very last I see. My eyes are dark. My tongue is still.

Wear chuckles somewhere in the night. His flowing cloak is decked with stars.

Sweetheart, have pity.

Perkin, hoist my hand again.

All's lost. All's found.

Farewell.

Reginald's last word.

THIS holy man ascended into Heaven in the spring of the seventeenth year of the reign of Our Sovereign Lord, Henry the Second, by the grace of God King of England, Duke of Normandy and Aquitaine and Earl of Anjou. He was one hundred and five years of age, having been born (as he himself reckoned it) the year before Duke William conquered the Saxons at Hastings. The manner of his parting was peaceful as befitted one who had lived for the last sixty years of his life at peace both with men and with God in a mean lodging which he had dug into the earth and covered with sod.

It was ever his custom to mortify his flesh in the river Wear even during the most frigid and intemperate days of winter, and it was after immersing himself therein one final time that he fell into a deep swoon, occasioned undoubtedly by the fluxion of the water which was still bitter cold from the abundance of melting snow and ice. As a result, he lost the powers both of speech and of perambulation. He was tended in his last hours by a rude servant whom he had befriended as a child, and although he could utter no word, lying there in the servant's arms, his lips were often seen to move as he endeavored to give utterance to various prayers and pious ejaculations.

In earlier times he had surrounded himself with serpents, nor did it in any way discomfit him that they were dangerous in the extreme and menaced all who came near with their venomous bites and hissing. With him, however, they were ever gentle, doing whatsoever he bade them and reclining between his feet like domestic pets or twining about his shins for warmth and companionship.

Two especially large members of this species appeared at the threshold of his cell toward nightfall of his final day upon this earth. Sensing that his end was not far off, however, they made no attempt to enter but kept vigil in the doorway until such time as the servant started forth to bear tidings of his master's demise, whereupon they stood aside to let him pass.

They remained at the door throughout the night as if on guard, and when his body was carried away to be prepared for burial the next morning, they followed at a respectful distance. Nor did they depart thence until he was laid to rest in the tomb which he had hewn out of hardest rock with his own hands and caused to be placed within the oratory which he had erected to the honor of the Blessed Virgin.

Great was the honor paid him by Bishop Hugh Pudsey, who, together with a host of canons, priests and monks, came out from Durham to celebrate mass on the occasion of his entombment. All who had known him gathered in solemn convocation to shed tears at the loss of so venerable and true a friend, but at the same time rejoicing that yet another soul had joined the blessed company of the elect in Heaven.

Of Godric's sanctity there can be no doubt. Although he himself was wont to deprecate them, none can count the deeds of charity that he wrought for the betterment of man nor the austerities he practised for the love of God. Although it has been said of him that like Our Lord he cleansed a leper, he was ever loth to lay claim to the working of any such miracles. In truth, he was a kind of miracle himself. Furthermore, since his death many who have prayed for him to intercede in their behalf in the courts of Heaven have had their petitions expeditiously granted, and there is one of his relics in particular—a rude wooden cross bound with hair which was found around his neck when he died— which is believed to have been most efficacious in the curing of numerous ills.

I myself, who was privileged to serve him during his latter years (when already his health was beginning to fail) can testify to the purity of his life, the magnanimity of his spirit, and, above all else, to his great humility. When at the instigation of Abbot Ailred of Rievaulx, of blessed memory, I initially undertook to record this history, he made violent objection, reviling himself most passionately and reciting in multitudinous detail the sins of his youth. He aspired thereby to demonstrate his unworthiness of any such biographical endeavor, but his better judgment at last prevailed, and in the end he gave his blessing to this work. Thus I set it forth now in confidence that the world will be greatly edified by the example of this most estimable man.

When old age overtook him and he endured the loss not only of bodily vigor but of all those whom he had once held most dear, he did not cease to praise God.

When he was assailed by doubts and fears and temptations, he was ever strong in Christ.

When death came for him at last, he did not quail before it but suffered it to bear him off as easily as a river bears off a fallen leaf.

Saint Godric, Father, pray for me. Pray for us all.

Amen.

Historical Note

In 1065 or thereabouts, Godric was born of Anglo-Saxon parents in Walpole (Norfolk). He became a peddler. Later he bought a half share in a ship and sailed as a merchant between England, Scotland, Denmark and Flanders. He made a pilgrimage to Rome accompanied by his aged mother, Aedwen. His father's name was Aedlward. Godric became for a time steward to a rich countryman. In 1101 he made a pilgrimage to Jerusalem. *The Dictionary of National Biography* states that "There is no need to doubt his identity with the *'Gudericus, pirata de regno Angliae'* with whom Baldwin I of Jerusalem, after his great defeat in the plains of Ramleh, sailed from Arsuf to Jaffa on 29 May 1102." About 1105 he sold all his goods, left home, and attempted to follow the life of a hermit, inspired perhaps by visits in seafaring days to the isle of Farne, once the home of Saint Cuthbert. He joined the hermit Elric at Wulsingham (Durham) until the latter's death in 1108. In Durham he acted as doorkeeper and bellringer at the church of Saint Giles and went to school with the choirboys at Saint Mary-le-Bow. Now over forty, he settled finally at Finchale, on the river Wear near Durham, on land belonging to Bishop Ranulf Flambard. From this day to the end of his life, he never left Finchale except three times and practised severe austerities.

In the first years of his retreat, his relatives came to visit him. His brother, William, was drowned in the Wear. His sister, Burcwen, after she had been a solitary herself at Finchale for a time, left to become a nun at Durham, where she died. His mother seems to have died at Finchale. Reginald, a monk of Durham, was commissioned by Ailred of Rievaulx to visit the old man with a view to writing his life. At first Godric refused to countenance a biography, but he eventually yielded and blessed the completed work when Reginald presented it to him. The passages that Reginald is described as reading to Godric in the next to last chapter of this book are free translations from his medieval Latin, as are also the words of self-condemnation that Godric speaks on page 21. Godric is credited with being the earliest known lyrical poet in English, and his work includes a hymn to the Virgin Mary which he is said to have set to music himself and a free rendering of which appears on page 21. Knowledge of future and distant events was attributed to him, and his love of and power over wild creatures was very remarkable, extending even to snakes, which he treated as domestic pets until they distracted him from his prayers. After a prolonged illness, during which he was nursed by Durham monks and a servant, he died on the 21st of May, 1170, which is his feast.

Frederick Buechner

Frederick Buechner was born in New York City. He was educated at Lawrenceville School, Princeton University, and Union Theological Seminary. In 1958 he was ordained to the Presbyterian ministry. He has written nine novels and a number of works of non-fiction including two volumes of meditations (*The Magnificent Defeat* and *The Hungering Dark*), *The Alphabet of Grace* (delivered as the Noble Lectures at Harvard), *Wishful Thinking: A Theological ABC, Telling the Truth: The Gospel as Tragedy, Comedy and Fairy Tale* (delivered as the Lyman Beecher lectures at Yale) and *Peculiar Treasures: A Biblical Who's Who,* illustrated by his daughter, Katherine A. Buechner. He lives in Vermont with his wife and family.